Emerging Challenges in Mergers and Acquisitions

Emerging Challenges in Mergers and Acquisitions

Edited by

Deeksha Malik and Aishwarya Choudhary

Cambridge Scholars Publishing

Emerging Challenges in Mergers and Acquisitions

Edited by Deeksha Malik and Aishwarya Choudhary

This book first published 2018

Cambridge Scholars Publishing

Lady Stephenson Library, Newcastle upon Tyne, NE6 2PA, UK

British Library Cataloguing in Publication Data
A catalogue record for this book is available from the British Library

ISBN (10): 1-5275-1632-6
ISBN (13): 978-1-5275-1632-8

TABLE OF CONTENTS

NOTE FROM THE EDITORS

Mergers and acquisitions (M&A) constitute an intrinsic part of business development. M&A can be seen in varied forms across the globe, such as value-chain optimisation, globalisation, consumer-base expansion or product diversification. Any entity's long-term success is dependent on its planned and strategized actions, which can be executed in any of the above-mentioned forms; however, for an M&A process to be effective, it needs to be analysed in terms of opportunity to transform, potential for reward and risk of danger. An ideal merger can be transformational for any entity, enabling it to widen its margin by virtue of economies of scale, entering new markets and adopting new technologies. On the other hand, the cost of a failed M&A transaction could be the destruction of shareholder value and of the business itself; therefore, a buoyant and profitable M&A deal is about stacking the odds in one's favour.

India has witnessed tremendous development in the area of M&A over the past few years. Of late, several big-ticket deals have been in the limelight. Acquisitions have been particularly successful, as exemplified by Flipkart's acquisition of eBay India, Axis Bank's acquisition of payments wallet FreeCharge and Ola's acquisition of Foodpanda, and India Inc. has been increasingly using this tool for hiring new talent, entering into new segments, technology and brands, among other things. With 944 deals, it is estimated that the M&A activity reached US$46.5 billion in 2017, which is a 165% increase from 2016. A Baker McKenzie report attributes this growth to the Indian government's targeted policies aimed at making the country a favourable investment destination. Indeed, with a liberalised foreign direct investment regime involving faster pace of approvals, simplification of the indirect tax structure due to introduction of the Goods and Services Tax, complete overhaul of the insolvency process for corporates under the Insolvency and Bankruptcy Code, 2016, and other initiatives under the "Make in India" programme, there is no looking back. India will continue to experience a boom in M&A, both in terms of the number of deals and the size of the transactions, especially in areas such as infrastructure, healthcare, financial services and e-commerce.

The law on M&A in India is young compared to other developed fields of law. It includes within its capacious content the rights of various stakeholders during an M&A deal, the distribution of the collective resources and the liability which can be cast on any stakeholder. There might not be any specific statute governing only M&A, but various aspects of M&A are dealt with in the Companies Act, 2013, the Income Tax Act, 1961, the Securities and Exchange Board of India (Substantial Acquisition of Shares and Takeovers) Regulations, 2011, the Securities and Exchange Board of India (Listing Obligations and Disclosure Requirements) Regulations, 2015, and so on. Further, with the advent of time and recent contemporary laws, there are various inter-linkages which cannot be catered to with a narrow understanding of the law. Each and every facet of an M&A deal needs to be studied from all viewpoints, be it labour law, insolvency law, securities and investment law, or anti-trust law, for all these considerations have a bearing on the mechanics of a deal.

This book is a compilation of the papers selected by the National Law Institute University, Bhopal, India (NLIU) as part of the NLIU Trilegal Summit on Mergers and Acquisitions, 2018, organised in association with Trilegal, one of the premier law firms in India. The Summit is an annual event wherein students from different law schools in India present their papers on niche issues in the area of M&A. In its 2018 edition, under the broad theme of *Emerging Challenges in M&A,* authors had the opportunity to delve into sub-themes such as anti-trust trends in M&A, M&A projections in the real estate market, impact of General Anti-Avoidance Rules on M&A, regulatory developments affecting M&A transactions, and M&A activity in the light of the new insolvency regime under the Insolvency and Bankruptcy Code, 2016. The various papers in the book and the treatment of the issues examined therein clearly reveal that the authors have deciphered the most intricate details involved in any M&A transaction. Every fundamental provision has been brought down to the most generic level, to enable clarity and understanding, looked at and explained in an articulate manner. There are various interesting and illuminating parts lying in the authors' works, which throw light on upcoming fusions and challenges in M&A. This book can be attributed to only the authors and their industrious energy and vigour.

CHAPTER I

DECRYPTING THE LIBERALISED FOREIGN DIRECT INVESTMENT POLICY AS A FACILITATOR OF CROSS-COUNTRY MERGERS AND ACQUISITIONS: MAXIMUM GOVERNANCE AND MINIMUM GOVERNMENT

ABHINANDAN JAIN AND DRISHMEET BUTTAR

Abstract

The incessantly evolving economic framework entails in its fold the increasing contribution of mergers and acquisitions (M&A). The same, in the contemporary corporate era, stands overhauled in the light of the adoption of a politically driven economic philosophy of maximum governance and minimum government, having been remarkably inducted in the extant policy framework. The present discussion is a novice and humble attempt at decrypting the upshots of the ceaselessly evolving foreign direct investment (FDI) regime of the country on cross-border M&A deals, specifically inbound transactions. In pursuance of the same, this work presents an exhaustive study of the recently staged FDI policy framework (II), while also emphasising its inputs in FDI-inducive sectors in terms of value and volume of inbound deals, underlining the news-making transactions (III). In consideration of the fact that an isolated evaluation of the consolidated FDI policy would be tantamount to unsound forecasts (thereby, conjectures), the compatibility between the extant FDI regime and foremost economic reforms in acting as catalysts in increasing cross-border M&A transactions is also the focus of analysis and assessment (IV). As a disclaimer, owing to the topic's dynamism, the predictions as expressed by the work of the authors are subject to changes in economic frameworks, both domestic and international.

Introduction

"Economic change creates winners and losers, even as society improves on a broader level."
—Robert Rubin, former United States Treasury Secretary

The vigorously evolving landscape of cross-border M&A has, of late, been under the globally casted watchful eyes of financial and economic geniuses. The on-going scrutiny is a natural genesis of the exponential growth and emergence that it has experienced in economies across the globe, to which India, in all certainty, is no exception. This stance stands reaffirmed by an increment of roughly 3% in the initial nine months of 2017—the greatest increase in terms of deal value since 2010, with inbound M&A activity having hit a decade high of $24.5 billion, up 61.6% from the previous year.[1] There is, however, much more to this figure than what meets the eye. Exceedingly cyclical, rhythmic and dynamic, cross-border M&A are subject to an economy's legally determined regulatory framework.

It is of immense importance to assess the robustness of the same in light of breakthrough measures in the form of a series of structural, banking, infrastructural and fiscal reforms of the current as well as preceding financial year (FY). This assessment mandates the worthy mention of the extant FDI Policy, which has subtly injected the optimum dosage of liberalisation and deregulation of the foreign investment regime, of which cross-country M&A form a substantial part. A novice assessment, thus, ensures that if FDI is the genus, inbound M&A transactions are the species. If favourable cross-border M&A are a means of achieving higher FDI, the FDI regulatory regime is the means of attaining a surge in such cross-border M&A deals.

In light of this, the present document is a humble attempt at decoding the repercussions of the ceaselessly evolving FDI regime of the country on cross-border M&A deals, particularly inbound transactions, by undertaking an exhaustive study of the newly staged FDI regime, while also emphasising its contribution to each specific sector in terms of value

---

[1] FE Bureau, "Mergers and Acquisitions Deal Value Highest Since 2010 in Jan-Sept Period at $43.2 Bn," *Financial Express,* October 7, 2017, http://www.financialexpress.com/industry/mergers-and-acquisitions-deal-value-highest-since-2010-in-jan-sept-period-at-43-2-bn/885531/.

and volume of inbound deals. In consideration of the fact that an isolated evaluation of the consolidated FDI policy would be tantamount to unsound forecasts (and therefore, conjectures), the compatibility between the extant FDI regime and foremost economic reforms in acting as catalysts in increasing cross-border M&A transactions will also be elucidated upon.

I. How "Unregulated" is the Regulatory Framework under the Reformed FDI Policy: Focal Features and Plausible Implications of Cross-Border M&A

A painstakingly exhaustive analysis of the contemporary global scenario shows the significant impact of the domestic FDI regime on cross-country M&A. Undeniably, the potential entrants are discouraged and rejected by an extensively regulated environment under the FDI regime.[2] A classic instance of state-controlled economy with a cumbersome bureaucracy, the FDI approval process in India has been perceived and documented as the major cause of concern and repulsion for foreign investors.[3] Involving numerous nominally distinct approval procedures for national and local agencies, this process is taxing and lengthier than that of other Asian economies, including Japan and China.[4] The deferrals and delays in the approval and implementation process of foreign investment deals is attributed to the undeniable existence of corruption and "red-tapism" in the Indian administrative fabric,[5] thereby hampering the potential of the Indian investment climate to facilitate cross-border M&A.

On the basis of this assessment, and seeking a steady and mounting momentum in inbound and outbound M&A activities in India, the Government of India has positioned the most radical sectors of the Indian economy under the "automatic approval route" in the lately consolidated FDI policies. Discerning between "automatic route" and "government

---

[2] "Economic and Other Impacts of Foreign Corporate Takeovers in OECD Countries," Organisation for Economic Co-operation and Development, 2007, https://www.oecd.org/daf/inv/investment-policy/40476100.pdf.

[3] "FDI Confidence Index," Global Business Policy Council: A.T. Kearney 7 (October 2004).

[4] Rohit Sachdev, "Comparing the Legal Foundations of Foreign Direct Investment in India and China: Law and the Rule of Law in the Indian Foreign Direct Investment Context," *Columbus Business Law Review*. BUS. L. REV. (August 2006): 209–11.

[5] Ajay Sharma, "Comparative Analysis of the Chinese and Indian FDI Regimes," *Chicago-Kent Journal of International and Comparative Law* 15, no. 3 (January 2015): 16.

route", it should be stated that the investment in the capital of resident entities by non-resident entities can be made without the prior approval of the government in the former, unlike the latter.[6] The foreign investment norms have further been eased by increasing the foreign investment limits across various sectors in anticipation of heightening the cross-country M&A activities in India. This notion is ideologically reaffirmed by contemporary research literature, which avers that the absence of capital controls facilitates the unrestricted funding of investments abroad, paving the way for cross-country acquisitions. Having "coincided with an increased attention to FDI protection and promotion",[7] liberalisation of the investment regime was hailed by the South-East Asian economies in the 1960s, followed by the rest of the Asian countries and Latin America in the 1980s and 1990s.[8]

---

[6] Consolidated FDI Policy of 2017, F. No. 5(1)/2017-FC-1, 2.1.20, Department of Industrial Policy and Promotion (2017), http://dipp.nic.in/sites/default/files/CFPC_2017_FINAL_RELEASED_28.8.17.pdf.

[7] Dirk Willem te Velde, "Foreign Direct Investment and Development: An historical perspective," *Overseas Development Institute,* January 30, 2006, https://www.odi.org/sites/odi.org.uk/files/odi-assets/publications-opinion-files/850.pdf, 10.

[8] te Velde, "Foreign Direct Investment and Development," 10.

Table showing comparative analysis of the consolidated FDI policies of 2015,[9] 2016[10] and 2017[11] on strategic sectors of the economy in terms of % of equity and entry route

S. No.	SECTOR	% OF EQUITY/ FDI CAP			ENTRY ROUTE		
		2015	2016	2017	2015	2016	2017
1.	Civil Aviation a. Airports (existing projects) b. Non-Scheduled Air Transport Service	100	100	100	Automatic up to 74%	Automatic up to 74%	Automatic (100%)
2.	Pharmaceuticals (Brownfield)	100	100	100	Government	Automatic up to 74%	Automatic up to 100%
3.	Defence	49	49	100	Government route up to 49% Above 49% to Cabinet Committee on Security (CCS)	Automatic up to 49% Above 49% under Government route	Automatic up to 49% Above 49% under Government route (*elimination of condition of access to "state-of-the-art" technology*)

[9] See Consolidated FDI Policy of 2015, F. No. 5(1)/2015-FC-1, Department of Industrial Policy and Promotion (2015), http://dipp.nic.in/sites/default/files/FDI_Circular_2015.pdf.

[10] See Consolidated FDI Policy of 2016, F. No. 5(1)/2016-FC-1, Department of Industrial Policy and Promotion (2016), http://dipp.nic.in/sites/default/files/FDI_Circular_2016%281%29.pdf.

[11] See Consolidated FDI Policy of 2017 (see n. 6).

4.	Finance a. Asset Reconstruction Companies b. Insurance	100 49	100 49	100 49	Automatic up to 49% Automatic up to 26%	Automatic Automatic	Automatic Automatic
5.	Trading of food products manufactured in India	-	-	100	-	-	Government approval route for trading, including through e-commerce
6.	LLP insectors where 100% FDI is allowed	100	100	100	Government	Automatic	Automatic
7.	Private Security Agencies	49	49	74	Government	Government	Automatic up to 49%

Additionally, the Single Brand Retail Trading (SBRT) sector has been substantially relaxed by the recently announced FDI policy of August 2017, which does away with the previous 70:30 rule, which demanded that an Indian single-brand retailer manufacture at least 70% of the products in-house and outsource the remaining 30% in order to qualify for FDI. Having unlocked the doors for products having "state-of-the-art" and "cutting-edge" technology for which local sourcing is impractical,[12] the new regime has also granted permission to SBRT entities operating through brick-and-mortar stores to undertake retail trading through e-commerce.[13]

Tactfully paving the way for cross-border M&A, the unanimous object of the tools of the "automatic approval route" and "liberalised capital control regime" for the aforementioned sectors is further expedited by parallel relaxations under the FDI policy of 2017. Specifically, they have stimulated the simplification of the process for establishing offices in India for the leading businesses in the defence, telecom, private security, and information and broadcasting sectors by eliminating the necessity for approval from the Reserve Bank of India in cases where the government approval or license/permission from the concerned ministry/regulator has already been granted.[14]

What is strikingly noteworthy is yet another development which has, in consideration of share swapping as a facilitator of cross-country M&A, remarkably injected liberalisation and deregulation into the investment process by "swap of share" under the FDI regime of 2016 (followed by that of 2017). It has hard-headedly excluded the requirement of government approval for investment in automatic-route sectors by way of swap of shares.[15]

Another emblematically exemplary reform under the regime of 2017 has been the abolishment of the 25-year ancient Foreign Investment Promotion Board (FIPB), thus slackening the aggressively regulated environment for 11 notified sectors requiring government approval which shall now be controlled by the concerned ministries/departments in consultation with the Department of Industrial Policy and Promotion (DIPP). Endorsing the "maximum governance and minimum government" model,[16] the government pondered and ultimately effected the abolition of

---

[12] See Consolidated FDI Policy of 2017, 5.2.15.3 (see n. 6).

[13] Consolidated FDI Policy of 2016, 5.2.15.3 (2)(f) (see n. 10).

[14] Consolidated FDI Policy of 2017, 3.7.2 (see n. 6).

[15] Consolidated FDI Policy of 2017, Annexure 4, 6 (see n.6).

[16] S. Arun, "Govt Approves Phasing Out Of 25-Year-Old Foreign Investment Promotion Board," *The Hindu,* May 24, 2017,

FIPB in view of the belief that, "Once the Board is history, red-tapism will shrink, ease of doing business will improve and investors will find India more attractive."[17] The rationale behind such an averment stands best explained by the logically expounded standpoint that heavily regulated business entry is associated with higher corruption, thus leading to weaker governance, which lowers the investment potential of an economy.[18]

In summary, liberalisation and deregulation of the FDI regime are reflective of a higher degree of market access and openness, which indeed are paramount determinants of outward FDI, of which cross-country M&A is, as repeatedly specified, an essential element.[19] The same can be substantiated by the policy landscape of India's Asian counterpart, Korea, one of the leading beneficiaries of M&A-associated FDI in the continent. The robust hike in the sales amounts of cross-border M&A from US$192 million in the year 1995 to US$10.1 billion in the year 1999 was largely credited to the incorporation of an "open-door policy" in the Korean FDI regime.[20] On an analogous appraisal and rationale, the policy makers in India have undertaken the similar route of relaxation under its existing FDI regime, so as to facilitate the process of cross-country M&A.

---

http://www.thehindu.com/business/Economy/cabinet-approves-abolition-of-fipb/article18561815.ece.

[17] Editor, "Abolishing FIPB: Red-tape Herring?" *The Hindu,* May 27, 2017, http://www.thehindu.com/opinion/editorial/red-tape-herring/article18586348.ece.

[18] S. Djankov and B. Hoekman, "Foreign Investment and Productivity Growth in Czech Enterprises," *World Bank Economic Review* 14, Issue 1 (January 2000): 49–64.

[19] Dimitrios Kyrkilis et al., "Macroeconomic Determinants of Outward Foreign Direct Investment," *International Journal of Social Economics* 30, no. 7 (July 2003): 831; Paula Neto, "The Macroeconomic Determinants of Cross Border Mergers and Acquisitions and Greenfield Investments," *FEP Working Papers,* no. 281 (June 2008): 9; N. Aminian et al., "Macroeconomic Determinants of Cross-Border Mergers and Acquisitions – European and Asian Evidence", International Conference at the University of Le Havre(September 2005); C. Culem, "The Locational Determinants of Direct Investment among Industrialized Countries," *European Economic Review* 32 (1988): 885–904; R. Biswas, "Determinants of Foreign Direct Investment," *Review of Development Economics* 6, no. 3 (2002): 492–504.

[20] Hwy-Chang Moon et al., "Cross-Border Mergers & Acquisitions: Case Studies of Korea, China, and Hong Kong," *Asia-Pacific Economic Corporation* (September 2003): 2.

II. Assessing the Influence of the FDI Regulatory Framework on Key Economic Sectors: An Insight into FDI-Stimulated News-Making Inbound Deals

Amalgamation of one entity with another is a cumbersome and subtle process, whether the entity is merging, acquiring or being acquired. The same process is bound to involve more intricacies and technical hitches when the concerned parties resolve to engage in a cross-border merger or acquisition. By virtue of the notification in section 234 of the Companies Act, 2013, with effect from April 13, 2017, it has now become plausible to undertake, in addition to an inbound merger (i.e., foreign company merging into an Indian company with the latter as the extant entity), an outbound merger (i.e., Indian company merging into a foreign company located in an approved jurisdiction with the latter as the extant entity), which hitherto was not legally recognised. Of late, cross-border deals have seen a considerable upsurge, especially in the years 2016 and 2017, owing to multifarious factors, *viz.* eased credit conditions, a stable capital market situation, liberalised FDI policies in 2016 and 2017, the Union Budget of 2016–17, and persistent improvement in economic policy reforms. The buoyant momentum and rise in the M&A value in cross-border activity can be assessed and deciphered from the impact on different sectors of the economy, which have been elucidated upon hereunder in light of the recently reformed FDI policy.

A. Infrastructure Sector

The infrastructure sector, in the past as well as in the near future, is unquestionably expected to be the focal point of concentration, being the engine of India's economic development and progress. The Indian infrastructure sector recorded deals worth approximately US$4 billion in 2016, the deal value surging by nearly 78% as compared to 2015.[21] Power, roads and renewable segments harnessed a substantial share, and, within that, 88% of the transactions which took place were via M&A.[22] Within

---

[21] "Transactions 2017: Inbound M&A Takes Center Stage," Ernst & Young, http://www.ey.com/Publication/vwLUAssets/ey-transaction-2017/$FILE/ey-transaction-2017.pdf.

[22] Shailaja Sharma, "Infrastructure Sector Sees Deals Worth $3.49 billion in FY17," *Livemint,* April 07, 2017, http://www.livemint.com/Companies/0B0ebU1CJ412AyYRv9JSKL/Infrastructure-sector-sees-deals-worth-349-billion-in-FY1.html.

infrastructure, the power division hogged the limelight as it collectively accounted for 53% of the total disclosed value and 86% of the M&A in the sector.[23] The power sector maintained its supremacy in the first quarter of 2017 as well, with its disclosed deal value of US$589.5 million out of the overall revealed US$647.4 million, depicting an augmentation in the infrastructure sector when compared to the same time period in 2016.[24]

During the previous three years, the FDI regime has undergone liberalisation, with relaxation in 87 FDI rules across 21 sectors, including civil aviation, defence, construction and development; the deal environment appears to be productive based on a strong economic outlook, accommodative economic policy and salutary capital markets, as also depicted in the datum above. The relaxed FDI regime in the civil aviation sector, enforceable from August 2017, for instance, has triggered the interest of Turkey's Celebi Aviation Holding in buying state-owned Air India's ground handling operations, as revealed by India's aviation secretary Rajiv Nayan Choubey.[25]

The renewable energy segment forms a dominant part of this sector. On June 30, 2016, the World Bank extended its largest-ever financial assistance in terms of solar energy by agreeing to invest US$1 billion in solar energy projects.[26] Domestically, in September 2016, the Adani Group set up the world's largest solar power plant in Tamil Nadu by investing approximately Rs. 4,550 crores.[27] Inasmuch as inbound deals are concerned, Sembcorp Green Infra, which is the subsidiary of a Singapore-based company, acquired a 74% stake in the Mulanur Renewable Energy

---

[23] "Recent Mergers & Acquisition in India," Bank Exams Today, July 14, 2017, http://www.bankexamstoday.com/2017/07/recent-mergers-and-acquisition-in-india.html.

[24] "Transactions Quarterly: A Perspective on the Indian Transactions Market January - March 2017," Ernst &Young, http://www.ey.com/Publication/vwLUAssets/ey-transaction-quarterly-1-q-17/$File/ey-transaction-quarterly-1-q-17.pdf.

[25] Reuters staff, "Deals of the Day—Mergers and Acquisitions," *Reuters,* September 8, 2017, https://in.reuters.com/article/deals-day/deals-of-the-day-mergers-and-acquisitions-idINL4N1LP3TM.

[26] "Solar Energy to Power India of the Future," World Bank, June 30, 2016, http://www.worldbank.org/en/news/feature/2016/06/30/solar-energy-to-power-india-of-the-future.

[27] Virendra Pandit, "Adani Dedicates to Nation World's Largest Solar Plant in TN," *The Hindu Business Line*, September 21, 2016, http://www.thehindubusinessline.com/companies/adani-dedicates-to-nation-worlds-largest-solar-power-plant-in-tn/article9131623.ece.

Private Limited for around Rs. 1.581 billion in August 2016.[28] With the aim of fructifying and habituating the use of renewable sources of energy, the Ministry of New and Renewable Energy is on a persistent mission offering incentives such as ones based on capital and interest, generation-based incentives, concessional finance, and fiscal incentives in order to encourage the private investors.[29]

Without a doubt, the Indian market is expanding at an incessant pace, the corollary of which is the unremitting upsurge in the demand for transportation and warehousing services, thereby breeding the potential for intensification in the logistics segment. The statistical figures are a testament to the same, as out of the 22 deals, six deals amounting to US$38 million in total had been completed in the first quarter of 2017.

The immediate outcome of the reformed FDI regime is thus corroborated by the increases in the deal volumes and values as also signified above, and, in view of the government engrossing itself in the infrastructure sector, the country is expected to be the recipient of investments via diverse economic means.

B. Oil and Gas Sector

In 2016 there was a tremendous upswing in the oil and gas sector, inasmuch as cross-border deals and their value are concerned, as evidenced from the conceded fact that inbound deals occupied the limelight by concluding transactions to the tune of US$12.936 million (4 deals), whereas outbound deals totalled US$5.46 million (5 deals), the value conquering the market landscape in comparison to preceding years.

The growth in the afore-stated sector is due primarily to the cross-country agreements betwixt companies of Indian and Russian origin, wherein the latter assumed the status of an acquirer in one deal, while

[28] "Sembcorp Green Infra Acquires Wind Power Assets in Tamil Nadu," Sembcorp Green Infra press release, August 8, 2016, http://www.sembcorp.com/en/media/384997/sembcorp-green-infra-acquires-wind-power-project-in-tamil-nadu.pdf.

[29] Press Information Bureau, "A New Dawn in Renewable Energy- India Attains 4th Position in Global Wind Power Installed Capacity; 46.33 GW grid-interactive power; 7,518 MW of grid-connected power; 1502 MW Wind power capacity added; Small hydro power capacity reaches 4323 MW, 92305 Solar Pumps installed, 38,000 crore Green Energy Corridor is being set up; Surya Mitra mobile App launched, Solar Tariff as low as Rs 3/unit," Ministry of New and Renewable Energy press release, December 18, 2016, http://pib.nic.in/newsite/PrintRelease.aspx?relid=155612.

positioning itself as the target nation in three outbound deals. On the inbound front, the deal in which a consortium led by Russia's national oil company, Rosneft, acquired a 98% stake in Essar Oil Ltd. for US$13 billion, the sale of which was concluded on August 21, 2017, has been termed the grandest foreign direct investment.[30] Insofar as the noteworthy outbound deals in this segment are concerned, they include, firstly, the acquisition of an additional 11% shares in JSC Vankorneft by ONGC Videsh, raising its percentage of shares up to 26% and, secondly, the consortium led by Oil India Ltd., in which a subsidiary company of Bharat Petroleum Corporation Ltd. (BPCL) successfully acquired a 29.9% stake in Taas Yuryakh and a 23.9% stake in Vankorneft from the Rosneft Oil Company.[31]

In an effort to encourage and captivate FDI and inbound transactions in the sector, the FDI policy has undergone liberalisation; henceforth, instead of seeking an approval from Foreign Investment Promotion Board, foreign direct investment under the automatic route, inasmuch as petroleum refining by Central Public Sector Enterprises is concerned, has been permitted with 49% foreign equity. In 2016, during April–November, India happened to be the recipient of US$76 million in FDI in this sector, which statistically was approximately 62% overhead in comparison to FDI inflows during the analogous period in the previous year (US$49 million).[32] In addition, the government authorises 100% FDI in upstream and private-sector refining projects.[33] These favourable policy measures would, in all likelihood, be able to stimulate cross-border transactions in an efficacious manner.

Keeping in mind the current scenario, the accomplishment of the affluent Rosneft-Essar transaction is likely to extend a fillip to the erstwhile mushrooming M&A landscape, with the FDI inflows having an optimistic impact across diverse sectors. The curiosity and faith demonstrated and

---

[30] ET Bureau, "Essar Oil Completes $13 Billion Sale to Rosneft-Led Consortium in Largest FDI Deal," *The Economic Times,* August 22, 2017, https://economictimes.indiatimes.com/markets/stocks/news/essar-oil-completes-sale-of-india-assets-to-rosneft-for-12-9-bn/articleshow/60154679.cms.

[31] Press Trust of India, "OVL completes acquisition of 11% additional stake in Vankor," *The Economic Times,* October 31, 2016, https://economictimes.indiatimes.com/industry/energy/oil-gas/ovl-completes-acquisition-of-11-additional-stake-in-vankor/articleshow/55153801.cms.

[32] "Annual Report 2016-2017," Ministry of Petroleum and Natural Gas, Government of India, 17–19, http://petroleum.nic.in/sites/default/files/AR16-17.pdf.

[33] "Oil & Gas," India Brand Equity Foundation, April 21, 2017, https://www.ibef.org/download/Oil-and-Gas-April-2017.pdf.

reposed by the oil-rich nations in securing the Indian market for production purposes, on account of a drop in the price of crude oil and other commodities, has endured to be the propelling factor in the rising of deal values. Relying upon the BP Statistical Review of World Energy's report, which considers India to be the leading nation in terms of oil consumption by 2035, and the statistical fact that it has outdistanced Japan to capture the rank of the third-largest oil consumer in the previous year, it can categorically be stated that inbound deals are bound to increase as investors envisage potential economic profitability in the approaching epoch in the oil and gas sector.

C. Pharmaceutical Sector

The Indian pharmaceutical industry has garnered an impeccable worldwide reputation for its expertise and proficiency in the generic medicines, low-cost manufacturing and research services, ranking third for volume and 14th in terms of value,[34] further constituting nearly 70–80% of the branded generics markets. In the aftermath of throwing open of the pharmaceutical sector to 100% FDI in 2001 and proactively familiarising itself with the conceptual and policy differences between "greenfield" and "brownfield" investments in 2011, the FDI regime of 2016 was further relaxed by relocating the latter (brownfield) from the government approval route to the automatic approval route for investment up to 74%.

Analysing the influence of the same on cross-country M&A deals, it is imperative to mention that in spite of the marginal decrease in the number of inbound deals from 11 (2015) to 9 (2016), a rampant rise in the aggregate inbound deal value from US$1.155 billion (2015) to US$2.099 billion (2016) is noteworthy.[35] The same accounts for the announcement and subsequent accomplishment of two large sterile injectable cross-border inbound deals, the first one being the revised key foreign investment from China in the Indian manufacturing asset, which is visible in the acquisition of a stake of approximately 74% in Gland Pharma (Hyderabad-based company) by the Chinese drug firm Fosun Pharma for

[34] Manish Panchal, Charu Kapoor, and Mansi Mahajan, "Success Strategies For Indian Pharma Industry in an Uncertain World," *Business Standard,* February 17, 2014, http://www.business-standard.com/content/b2b-chemicals/-114021701557_1.html.

[35] "Transactions 2017," Ernst & Young.

US$1.1 billion on September 18, 2017.[36] The second deal was one wherein Ahmedabad-based pharma player Claris Lifesciences Ltd. was acquired for US$625 by Baxter International Inc. (US) on July 28, 2017.[37] The datum from Grant Thornton Advisory Pvt. Ltd has completely overturned the estimations of a speculated boost in 2017, asserting that until September 2017 there have been 27 M&A deals in the pharma and healthcare sector, valued at $719 million,[38] which is much lower than the 34 deals, valued at $2.675 billion, that took place in the first three quarters of 2016. This is credited to the overpowering influence of recently adopted financial alterations, chief among which is the implementation of the Goods and Services Tax in August 2017, justifying the "wait and watch" approach of the foreign investors, thus subduing the continued impact of the relaxed FDI regime of 2016.

Deliberating upon the strategic surge in the above-analysed scenario of 2016 in the light of that year's liberalised FDI regime, an upswing in inbound M&A deals in the fourth quarter (Q4) of 2017 and subsequent year is foreseeable, or, more accurately, perceptible on account of an increase in the FDI limit from 74% to 100% under the automatic route with effect from August 28, 2017. This standpoint stands remarkably confirmed by the news-breaking inauguration of Q4 by the acquisition of the domestic business of Ahmedabad-based Unichem Laboratories by Torrent Pharma for Rs. 3,600 crores.[39] Envisioned to swell to US$55 billion (or beyond) by 2020 at the current pace, it is unequivocally averred

---

[36] News Desk, "Fosun Pharma to Buy 74% Stake in Gland for $1.09 Billion," *Business Fortnight,* September 19, 2017, http://businessfortnight.com/fosun-pharma-to-buy-74-stake-in-gland-for-1-09-billion/.

[37] *Business Line*, "Claris Sells Global Generic Injectables Business to Baxter for $625 mn," *The Hindu Business Line,* July 28, 2017, http://www.thehindubusinessline.com/companies/claris-sells-global-generic-injectables-business-to-baxter-for-625-mn/article9792328.ece.

[38] P. B. Jayakumar, "Larger Merger and Acquisitions Back in Indian Pharma," *Business Today,* November 6, 2017, http://www.businesstoday.in/sectors/pharma/large-merger-and-acquisitions-back-in-indian-pharma/story/263399.html.

[39] Divya Rajgopal, "Torrent Pharma Walks Away with Unichem's Domestic Business for Rs. 3,600 Crore," *The Economic Times,* November 8, 2017, https://economictimes.indiatimes.com/industry/healthcare/biotech/pharmaceuticals/torrent-pharma-to-buy-unichem-labs-india-business-for-558-million/articleshow/61489554.cms.

that the pharmaceutical market may, contrariwise, be depressed in a "pessimistic scenario characterized by regulatory controls."[40]

D. Telecommunication Sector

In the wake of heightened competition and mounting consolidation in the telecom sector, the mergers and acquisition deals have witnessed a conspicuous upsurge in the preceding two years. In 2016, insofar as the telecom sector is concerned, 19 M&A deals have been transacted, the inbound deal activity hovering at an approximate value of US$1.083 billion.[41] The ballooning growth of data consumption, newly issued guidelines permitting the mobile phone companies to trade spectrum among themselves, and the need to survive the cut-throat environment brought on by Reliance Jio (acquisition of Tikona Digital's 4G airwaves by Bharti Airtel for US$244.5 million to compete with Jio and Vodafone-Idea Cellular) are positioned to be the major factors behind the escalating deals in relation to the spectrum acquisition. The same stands proven by the promising beginning to the first quarter of FY17, wherein the sector commandeered deals worth US$13.6 billion (the deal of Vodafone-Idea dominating the share percentage of US$11.6 billion), as compared to US$60 million a year ago.

The consolidation wave gaining momentum in 2016 has undauntedly driven the deal activity in the telecommunications sector in the current year as well, which can be evidenced from the statistical figure of the third quarter, clearly depicting that, despite a slowdown in the overall M&A activity, the telecom sector remained the most industrious and agile division, witnessing a 115% surge in the initial nine months from the corresponding period in FY16. As consolidation and sustainability in the sector occupies the centre stage, the FDI policy retains the 100% cap in telecom services with the subscriber base revealing a vigorous growth, and exponential inflows are expected from foreign investors; as a consequence of the latter, the inbound deals are likely to be the preferred mode of foreign direct investment.

The hike in the velocity of FDI in the telecom sector is already perceptible from the noteworthy factual situation, as recorded in the

---

[40] Vikas Bhadoria, Ankur Bhajanka, Kaustubh Chakraborty, and Palash Mitra, "India Pharma 2020: Propelling access and acceptance, realising true potential," McKinsey & Company report, http://online.wsj.com/public/resources/documents/McKinseyPharma2020ExecutiveSummary.pdf.

[41] "Transactions 2017," Ernst & Young.

government statistics, clearly showing the growth of the overseas funds in the telecom sector, which is three times larger than the preceding fiscal year, touching the US$10 billion mark in the initial three quarters of 2016–17. The ground-breaking inbound deal in the sector is Kohlberg Kravis Roberts & Co's massive investment to the tune of US$948 million in Bharti Infratel Ltd. for a 10.3% stake.[42] Of late, the American Tower Company (ATC) has struck an agreement with Vodafone and Idea Cellular for acquiring their mobile tower assets, which have an estimated value of Rs. 7,850 crores. Post-acquisition, ATC is bound to be graded as the second-biggest standalone mobile tower company, with a portfolio of 80,000 towers. As a matter of fact, India's telecom industry is the second-largest worldwide in terms of the number of subscribers, thereby showcasing the potentiality of the telecom market.

E. Financial Services Sector

In 2016, the financial services sector reached its peak by recording its highest ever M&A activity, both in terms of number and value. A total of 91 deals were announced, within which outbound and inbound deals were 7 and 12 in number, respectively. Within the sector, the fundamental segments included insurance (11 deals of US$3.3 billion), non-banking financial companies (NBFC) (27 deals of US$100 million), payment solutions (8 deals of US$130 million) and capital markets (12 deals of US$83 million). An unprecedented boost in the volume and value of inbound deals in the insurance sector, particularly health, is characterised by the liberalised FDI regime of 2016; for example, an increase in the limit on FDI under the automatic route from 26% to 49% under the consolidated FDI policy of 2016 translated into the purchase of an additional stake of 23.7% for US$24 million by German firm Munich Re in Apollo Munich Health Insurance, eventually raising the stake to 49%.[43] Under the 2016 policy, 100% FDI had been assented to through the automatic route for 18 specified NBFC activities, whereas the rules adopted under the policy of

---

[42] The Economic Times, "India Inc seals deals worth $17.9 billion in Q1 2017: Report," April 19, 2017, https://economictimes.indiatimes.com/news/company/corporate-trends/india-inc-seals-deals-worth-17-9-billion-in-q1-2017-report/articleshow/58260904.cms.

[43] Shilpy Sinha, "Munich Re to buy additional 23.27% stake in Apollo Munich Health Insurance for Rs. 163 crore," *The Economic Times*, January 27, 2016, https://economictimes.indiatimes.com/industry/banking/finance/munich-re-to-buy-additional-23-27-stake-in-apollo-munich-health-insurance-for-rs-163-crore/articleshow/50734599.cms.

2017 have further broadened the remit by allowing overseas investment in financial activities beyond the specified NBFC activities under the automatic route. In spite of the continued liberalised FDI policy framework carried forward from 2016 to 2017, the financial sector underwent a downturn with a 51% decline in the value of M&A deals in the first nine months from the previous FY,[44] credited to co-existing regulatory changes acting as dispelling factors. What single-handedly drove the banking sector in FY2017 was the National Multi Commodity Exchange's merger with the Indian commodity exchange, creating India's third biggest commodity exchange.[45]

III. Analyzing the Regulatory Measures as Enablers or Inhibitors of the FDI Policy in Surging Inbound M&A Deals

In light of the ever-evolving landscape of the Indian economy, an isolated evaluation of the consolidated FDI policy would lead to flawed forecasts and estimations. On the policy forefront, for instance, numerous government initiatives like "Skill India", "Make in India", "Start Up India", "Digital India" and "Stand Up India" are undeniably complementing the relaxed and supportive FDI regime, thus assigning a favourable outlook to inbound investments into the country. In corroboration, the start-up sector contributed 23% of M&A volumes in January-August 2017.

It becomes significant to understand the correlation between the FDI policy and the macroeconomic environment measures so as to determine whether the latter supplements the former as catalysts in boosting the cross-border M&A transactions; this necessitates a recap of a host of structural, banking, infrastructural and fiscal reforms of the current as well as the preceding FY.

Enactment of the Insolvency and Bankruptcy Code, 2016: Attempting to assess the compatibility between the FDI policy and the Insolvency and Bankruptcy Code, 2016 (IBC) in increasing the volume and value of cross-

---

[44] FE Bureau, "Mergers and acquisitions deal value highest since 2010 in Jan-Sept period at $43.2 bn," *Financial Express,* October 7, 2017, https://www.financialexpress.com/industry/mergers-and-acquisitions-deal-value-highest-since-2010-in-jan-sept-period-at-43-2-bn/885531/.

[45] Niti Kiran, "M&A values in July lowest in 73 months: Grant Thornton," *Business Today,* August 17, 2017, http://www.businesstoday.in/current/deals/m-and-a-values-in-july-lowest-in-73-months-grant-thornton/story/258529.html.

border M&A transactions, a dual-faceted moot originates. In accordance with the globally-suggested "creditor in possession" approach with an expeditious resolution process, the recently consolidated law on insolvency and bankruptcy is envisioned to enhance the inbound investment in asset reconstruction companies by strategically supplementing the FDI policies of 2016 and 2017; this has pragmatically placed this sector under the automatic approval route. The same is sought to be further augmented by the Banking Regulation (Amendment) Act, 2017, authorising the Reserve Bank of India (RBI) to direct banking companies to resolve required stressed assets by commencing the insolvency resolution process,[46] followed by the announcement of various relaxations to ease transactions involving distressed companies by the Securities and Exchange Board of India on June 21, 2017.[47] A paradoxical standpoint, however, asserts otherwise by claiming that the provision for review and reversal of undervalued transactions on a subjective determination of fraudulent debtors[48] austerely attacks the underlying idea behind the reformed FDI regime, revolving around liberalisation, deregulation and red-tape herring. The same is coupled with the "un-exempted" payment of stamp duty and other statutory costs in relation to acquisition of assets. Dubious, as it evidently is, to ascertain which of the two annotations would eventually subsist, the forthcoming years are eagerly awaited to witness the fate of the distressed cross-border M&A in India, in light of the disputed stance of the IBC as either an enabler or an inhibitor of the liberalised FDI regime.

Demonetisation and the digitisation thereof: The investment-receptive FDI regime in India in the sector of "e-commerce activities" has been complemented remarkably by the oft-debated state and structural measure of demonetisation, having taken the Asia-Pacific sub-continent by storm in the preceding year. Effecting a cashless economy, demonetisation is anticipated to reduce the cross-country M&A deals in the short term in businesses based on the "cash and delivery" payment method, thus overpowering the continued benefits of the liberalised FDI regime. Contrariwise, an observably significant implication of demonetisation is digitisation, warmly welcomed by two strategic sectors—finance and retail trading—and furthered by government initiatives such as Digital India. Catalysing "mobile banking for accessing payment, savings, insurance,

[46] The Banking Regulation Act, No. 10 of 1949, sec. 35AB, inserted by the Banking Regulation (Amendment) Act, No. 30 of 2017.

[47] Zeba Siddiqui and Abhirup Roy, "SEBI tightens rules for offshore derivatives," *Thomson Reuters (India),* June 21, 2017, https://www.reuters.com/article/india-sebi-derivatives/sebi-tightens-rules-for-offshore-derivatives-idINKBN19C1ID.

[48] The Insolvency and Bankruptcy Code, No. 31 of 2016, sec. 49.

credit services and micro-finance",[49] the financial services have been manifestly digitised, and thus the current "fintech" space is forecasted to attract massive cross-country M&A transactions. This stance is supported by the news-making acquisition of Citrus Pay, a Mumbai-based payments technology player, by South African Naspers' PayU for US$130 million in an all-cash deal, thus enabling the latter to add more than 30 million people to its user base.[50] Also, a deal-making incentive in the e-retail arena is anticipated in the long run on account of demonetisation, further eased and supplemented by the FDI policy measure of allowing SBRT entities to operate through brick-and-mortar stores for the purpose of retail trading through e-commerce. The injection of digitisation by demonetisation, which has perceptibly inoculated the already liberalised FDI regime (permitting investment up to 100% under the automatic approval route in the e-commerce sector), is expected to bolster up the value and volume of cross-country M&A deals in the long run on a "digitally constructed platform".

Implementation of the Goods and Services Tax: Broadening the sectoral-confined analysis to a cumulative standpoint, light must be shed on major fiscal reforms because they have an all-pervasive impact on inbound deals in all the sectors of the economy. Stimulatingly, the eighth month of FY17 saw the simultaneous implementation of the consolidated FDI regime and the Goods and Services Tax (GST), the most notable fiscal measure of all phases. In breach of the notional expectation of coherence between the two regulatory measures in increasing the volume and value of inbound deals, the latter instead overpowered and diluted the impact of the former. To put it across simply and statistically, the current September quarter drove transaction values to their lowest point in 32 quarters, standing at $2,142 billion with only 32 transactions.[51] The month of August recorded a 46% decline in the value of transactions from the corresponding period in the preceding year on account of reduced inbound deals because of the "wait and watch mode" of the investors checking the

---

[49] "Transactions 2017," Ernst & Young.

[50] Biswarup Gooptu and Arun Kumar, "Naspers-owned PayU snaps up Citrus Pay for $130 million in one of the largest fintech deals in India," *The Economic Times,* September 15, 2016, https://economictimes.indiatimes.com/small-biz/startups/naspers-owned-payu-snaps-up-citrus-pay-for-130-million-in-one-of-the-largest-fintech-deals-in-india/articleshow/54321363.cms.

[51] PTI, "Mergers and Acquisitions hit by demonetization, GST rollout: Grant Thornton," *The Hindu Business Line,* October 13, 2017, http://www.thehindubusinessline.com/companies/mergers-and-acquisitions-hit-by-demonetisation-gst-roll-out-grant-thornton/article9902081.ece.

progress of GST implementation.[52] The FDI policy's inability to keep the surge in inbound M&A transactions intact is thus credited solely to the apprehensive atmosphere generated by GST implementation.

The first two quarters of the current FY deserve to be applauded for considerably elevating M&A in the initial nine months, remarkably substantiating the coordinated operation of the FDI regime in 2016 and other regulatory reforms. Regardless of the sudden dip in the M&A transactions in Q3 for reasons explicated above, the drop is short-lived, for tomorrow's predicted hike is reflected in the Ease of Doing Business Index for 2018, in which India has historically hopped 30 spots from the preceding year to 100th rank this year.[53]

V. Conclusion and Recommendations

In an attempt to accentuate and keep the already mounting cross-country transactions intact, a host of suggestions are proposed to be incorporated into the current FDI policy and the generic regulatory framework. The framework prescribing different foreign investment norms for brownfield and greenfield investment in the pharmaceutical sector should also be introduced in other key sectors of the economy so as to liberalise the investment regime in the former to eliminate trepidations in the latter. The same would, in consequence, amount to a robust boost in inbound transactions.

So as to supplement the FDI policies of 2016 and 2017, which have pragmatically placed the investment in asset reconstruction companies under the automatic approval route with a 100% equity cap, section 49 of the IBC should be amended, for it subjects undervalued transactions to cumbersome judicial scrutiny on the speculated existence of a fraudulent debtor.

With a view to providing fillip to inbound M&As by foreign investors, it is of extreme pertinence for the Indian government to direct their measures and policies towards innovation and upgradation of technology, as technological scarcity has vastly hindered the overseas companies in

---

[52] PTI, "M&A deal value plunges by 46%, firms cautious after GST rollout," *The Hindu Business Line*, September 12, 2017, http://www.thehindubusinessline.com/economy/ma-deal-value-plunges-by-46-firms-cautious-after-gst-rollout/article9856092.ece.

[53] "India makes it to Top 100 in 'ease of doing business'," *The Hindu Business Line,* October 31, 2017, http://www.thehindubusinessline.com/economy/policy/india-makes-it-to-top-100in-ease-of-doing-business/article9935450.ece.

investing in capital-intensive industries, thereby keeping this segment in a virtually dormant state when viewed with respect to its potentiality.

Like the liberalised SBRT sector, the investment limit of 51% under the government approval route in the Market Brand Retail Trading (MBRT) sector should also be relaxed so as to facilitate increased inbound transactions in the retail trading sector and exploit the advantageous position that it is in following the abolition of FIPB.

The current intellectual property regime in our country is much weaker when compared to other countries such as the US and China. For this reason, having a robust and protective IP system in place would encourage innovative companies to transmit their technologies and business methods, thereby sharply augmenting the FDI inflows and inbound deals, especially in the Indian pharmaceutical sector, which undeniably would increase common peoples' access to advanced pharmaceutical drugs.

The on-going momentum in the M&A activity is likely to continue as the economy progresses through 2017, notwithstanding the short-term lull that the implementation of GST or demonetisation has exerted. The present age has revolutionised the economy by undertaking a liberalised yet governed framework, and the current FDI policy in its endeavour to boost the cross-country M&A is no exception.

CHAPTER II

THE INTERSECTION OF INSOLVENCY LAW AND COMPANY LAW: A PERSPECTIVE ON MERGER AND AMALGAMATION

SHASHANK CHADDHA

Abstract

With the enactment of the Insolvency and Bankruptcy Code, 2016, there has been a paradigm shift in the way corporates function, especially in creditor-tasked transactions. With the advent of a creditor-friendly regime, other stakeholders in a company undergoing the corporate insolvency resolution process unfortunately have to take a back seat. This paper highlights such instances, specifically with reference to the provisions and mandates of the Companies Act, 2013. The paper has been divided into five parts. The first part deals with the introduction to the paper. The second part, taking it further, deals with some pertinent questions which the author thinks should be considered for the debate in light of the lack of clarity on some provisions of the Code. The third part moves to the advanced stage of a resolution plan and the point where it clashes with the Companies Act, 2013, and it discusses the preferred treatment given to the creditors over the shareholders of the corporate debtor while deciding the latter's fate. In order to provide a contrast to the situation of our Code, the fourth part presents the situation in other jurisdictions. Lastly, with the fifth part, the paper concludes by suggesting changes in the law; the author has suggested the exact provisions which may be inserted in order to synchronise the Code with the Companies Act, 2013.

KEYWORDS: Exit option; shareholders; scheme of arrangement; Insolvency and Bankruptcy Code; UK Insolvency Act; US Bankruptcy Code.

I. Introduction

The previous year saw an overhaul in the corporate landscape in the country wherein various legislative reforms were introduced in order to restructure the position of India as a hub of foreign investment. Over a year into the enactment and application of the new insolvency regime of the country—the Insolvency and Bankruptcy Code, 2016 (IBC)—there has been extensive deliberation over the effects and effectiveness that the provisions of the IBC ensue. One of the main objectives of this new law is to codify and consolidate all the existing laws which dealt with insolvency and bankruptcy in order to create certainty and efficiency, and to bring the procedure under the umbrella of one judicial body—the National Company Law Tribunal (NCLT) or the National Company Law Appellate Tribunal (NCLAT). This new law has been a result of extensive analysis of the already developed insolvency practice in the United States and the United Kingdom. As observed in the Bankruptcy Law Reforms Committee's (BLRC) Report:

> A comprehensive and consistent treatment of bankruptcy and insolvency for all these is an essential ingredient of India's rise into a mature market economy. The draft "Indian Financial Code", by Justice Srikrishna's Financial Sector Legislative Reforms Commission, covers the failure of financial firms. The present Committee has taken up the task of drafting a single unified framework which deals with bankruptcy and insolvency by persons other than financial firms.[1]

The intention of the Parliament has therefore been to have a clean modern law which is a simple, coherent and effective answer to the problems faced under Indian conditions.[2] At the outset, the BLRC Report talked about all major aspects which concern a comprehensive insolvency law; however, it did fall short of accounting for various peculiar, and substantially important, issues which have now come up as a result of practical difficulties in implementing the intent and provision of the IBC. This essay highlights the practical lacunae which are bound to occur and argues that the present IBC does not account for some of these. What is more alarming is the absence of clarity on such situations by any law currently in force. As a result, this paper, after identifying the gaps present in the present IBC and the possible conflicts which the provisions of the

---

[1] The Insolvency and Bankruptcy Board of India, *The Report of the Bankruptcy Law Reforms Committee Volume I: Rationale and Design* (November 2015): 12, http://ibbi.gov.in/BLRCReportVol1_04112015.pdf (*BLRC Report*).

[2] *BLRC Report*, Executive Summary.

new law might create, suggests the possible solutions that could be adopted or should have been adopted by the Parliament—or the Central Government, in the case of the recently promulgated Ordinance—to address such situations. The primary aspect of this conflict can be seen in the effect that the IBC has on the mandatory provisions of company law and those of securities law. Such instances of conflict, as highlighted in the next part, stem from the role and power of those who are termed as "legal entities" of the IBC.

II. Effect of Moratorium

The BLRC Report—the primary source for deriving the intention of the Parliament in case of the IBC—states that there are some institutions which form the core of the functioning of the IBC,[3] such as the Interim Resolution Professional (IRP), the Resolution Professional (RP) and the Committee of Creditors (CoC). Due to the roles that such entities perform, as mandated by the IBC, the actions that are taken under the IBC result in substantial dilution of the provisions of the Companies Act, which is the focus of this part.

After an insolvency petition has been admitted by the NCLT, the moratorium period commences,[4] which results in the suspension of the board[5] of the corporate debtor—the company against whom the petition has been instituted. Consequently, when an IRP is appointed, that IRP performs various duties ranging from entering into contracts on behalf of the corporate debtor to issuing instructions to the personnel thereof. As a residuary power, the IRP can take all such steps as may be necessary to run the corporate debtor as a going concern.[6] Once that IRP/RP is vested with the powers of the board of the corporate debtor,[7] it becomes imperative to assess the level of competence of that IRP in terms of the decision-making ability of a company.

In a practical setting, the scope of the application of "moratorium" requires identification. As per the BLRC Report, there exists a "calm period" enabling creditors and debtors to negotiate the viability of the entity. In this calm period (moratorium), a regulated insolvency professional

---

[3]*BLRC Report*, 73.

[4] The Insolvency and Bankruptcy Code of 2016 (IBC), No. 31 of 2016, section 13.

[5] M/s. Innoventive Industries Ltd. v. ICICI Bank & Anr., [2017] 205 CompCas 23, ¶52; In Re: Vimal Prakash Dubey, (Order of the Insolvency and Bankruptcy Board of India – 14.03.2017).

[6] IBC, section 20(2)(e).

[7] IBC, section 20(2)(e).

controls the assets under the supervision of an adjudicating authority.[8] Considering that the institution of moratorium prohibits initiation of suits or continuation of pending proceedings,[9] the question that arises with respect to the application of section 14 of the IBC is whether it also affects the on-going/pending application of approval of a scheme of arrangement which the concerned company—the corporate debtor—had filed before the commencement of the moratorium period. The logical conclusion that flows from section 14 attempts to address this situation at first; however, the IBC's conceptual understanding of a "moratorium" falls short of the given hypothetical situation. The purpose of a moratorium is essentially to hold off on all the pending disputes by or against the corporate debtor; however, whether the filing of an application seeking approval for a scheme of arrangement falls under the definition of pending litigation/suits/proceedings is a grey area. If it does, the conclusion then indicates that even the application filed for a scheme of arrangement is stopped or prohibited from continuing. The gap regarding the application of the IBC's provisions in the scenario provided arises when we consider the practical aspects of this situation. Given that the pending proceedings will be prohibited from continuation, what requires examination is whether, once the IRP takes charge of the debtor company, the prohibited scheme of arrangement, which was filed after the approval of the concerned stakeholders as per the Companies Act, continues or is considered by the CoC in the advanced stage concerning the approval of a resolution plan for reviving the debtor company. For this, the point as to whether an application filed for approval of a scheme of arrangement will be considered as "proceedings" for the purposes of section 14 of the IBC becomes moot. An indicative answer to this can be seen from the provisions of the NCLT Rules, 2016, wherein the word "application" means "proceedings".[10] Similarly, the definition of "transferred application/petition" also means any "proceeding".[11] This shows that the word "proceedings" in reference to NCLT has a wide definition, and, therefore, the natural interpretation of the word "proceedings" under section 14 of the IBC may also include any application filed with the NCLT.

Moreover, considering that the scheme under consideration will also have another company, the implications of prohibiting the continuation of

---

[8] *BLRC Report*, at 74 (see n. 1).

[9] IBC, section 14.

[10] The National Company Law Tribunal Rules of 2016 (NCLT Rules, 2016), rule 2(5).

[11] NCLT Rules, 2016, rule 2(29).

the pending proceedings—in the present case, the filing of the scheme of arrangement—may have an adverse effect as the other company may have altered its position from the one it held prior to the commencement of the insolvency petition. The answer to addressing this practical difficulty therefore lies in interpreting the "proceedings" in a manner which provides enough breathing space for such proceedings which do not involve any manner of opposition from any party. This is particularly crucial in light of the intended measures that are pragmatically suggested at the advanced stage of the resolution plan. Although there has been just one case in which a resolution plan involving a scheme of arrangement has been approved at the time the present paper was authored,[12] the gist of the argument is that a scheme of arrangement—which has been on-going—should not be prohibited by virtue of section 14. If the proposed scheme makes the debtor company commercially viable again, then the further process of continuing with the insolvency petition should be done away with, as the intended result of an insolvency resolution petition has already been achieved.

III. Resolution Plan—The Rigours of Compliances

As the corporate insolvency resolution process proceeds to the advanced stages, the next crucial stage is the meeting of the CoC and the approval of a Resolution Plan (Plan). After the formation of the CoC, the IRP/RP prepares an information memorandum[13] for the purposes of inviting proposals from resolution applicants who subsequently put forth their respective resolution plans for deliberation before the CoC comprising of financial creditors.[14] Such resolution plans contain measures which, according to the resolution applicant, will further the revival objective of the IBC and will be effective in restoring the operations and soundness of the corporate debtor. This part of the article deals with the compliances which are inherently required in case the approved resolution plan proceeds to formulate a scheme of arrangement (merger or amalgamation) as the revival plan for the debtor company.

Recently, the Ministry of Corporate Affairs (MCA), Government of India, released a clarification stating that the approval of a Plan containing provision for a scheme of arrangement from the NCLT/NCLAT shall be

[12] Synergies-Dooray Automotive Limited v. Edelweiss Asset Reconstruction Company and Ors., (NCLT, Hyderabad – 02.08.2017), (2018) 1 CompLJ 89.

[13] IBC, section 29.

[14] IBC, section 21(2).

construed to have been consented to by the shareholders of the debtor company, and that it shall be binding on all stakeholders including shareholders. Considering that there will be a "deemed consent" by this clarification as far as the consent of shareholders is concerned, this clarification does more harm than good. The following paragraphs attempt to explain the effects of such deemed consent.

A) Purpose of Prior Approval of Shareholders

In company law jurisprudence, one of the important components of a company—public or private—is the entity of shareholder(s), and this entity has been conferred various powers including that of removal of a director.[15] A brief perusal of the provisions relating to merger and amalgamations[16] would show the importance of a general meeting which is primarily convened for the purpose of obtaining shareholders' approval on the scheme. In support of this argument, reference must also be made to the *Report of the Standing Committee, Lok Sabha, Parliament of India,* which, *inter alia,* dealt with the proposal of eliminating the meeting of shareholders to decide on the scheme of merger and amalgamation. The Committee, therein, commented that irrespective of whether there is a unanimous consent of shareholders on the proposal of the intended scheme, the meeting should be convened. The meeting is required to be held in order that the information about the merger/amalgamation is made known to the members;[17] therefore, the importance of this meeting of shareholders is evident from the Report of the Committee. Moreover, the NCLT, in *JVA Trading Pvt. Ltd. and C&S Electric Limited,*[18] has said that it does not possess the power of dispensing with the meeting of shareholders; accordingly, it is submitted that if dispensing with the shareholders' meeting cannot be done under the Companies Act, it must

[15] Kurz v. Holbrook, 989 A.2d 140 (Del. Ch. 2010); Hockessin Community Center, Inc. v. Swift, 59 A.3d 437 (Del. Ch. 2012).

[16] The Companies Act of 2013, No. 18 of 2013, Chapter XV, COMPROMISES, ARRANGEMENTS AND AMALGAMATIONS (sections 230 to 240).

[17] The Companies Bill, 2011: 57th Report, Standing Committee on Finance, Ministry of Corporate Affairs, Government of India, (June 2012), http://www.prsindia.org/uploads/media/Company/Companies_Bill_%20SC%20Report%202012.pdf.

[18] In the matter of JVA Trading Pvt. Ltd. and C&S Electric Limited (NCLT, Principal Bench, 13.01.2017), accessed December 5, 2017, https://indiacorplaw.in/wp-content/uploads/2017/01/JVA20Trading 20Pvt20Ltd..pdf.

also not be done under the IBC, due to the purpose of the meeting. As general corporators of a company,[19] shareholders should be made aware of the implications of any such scheme which has the potential to affect their vested interests in the company.

In the past, the judicial approach has been very critical of any step that might be oppressive to shareholders, especially minority shareholders.[20] Dispensing with an essential meeting of the shareholders substantially dilutes the mandatory requirement of having a fair scheme, and it may also prove to be oppressive to some shareholders, if not to all of them.

B) Dilution of Exit Option

In order to balance the interests of minority shareholders, an "exit option" is mandatorily to be provided to those shareholders who vote against the scheme—the dissenting shareholders. A proper and fair scheme gives the remaining shareholders an exit option.[21] In fact, the Companies Act, 2013, under section 230(7), mandates providing such an exit opportunity to the dissenting shareholders. This option is in furtherance of "the intent … to ensure fair valuation of such shares/ assets/ properties and to protect interest of non-promoter shareholders."[22]

When we consider the situation of the IBC in light of the MCA Clarification, however, the mandate of entitlement of dissenting shareholders stands diluted, as there is no way to determine the approval or dissention of any shareholders because in order to have these categories there has to be a general meeting of the company, and this is dispensed with by the operation of the provisions of the IBC. Considering that with the operation of section 31(1) an approved Plan shall be binding on the corporate debtor and its employees, members, creditors, guarantors and, crucially, other stakeholders, it is evidently and manifestly inequitable that a Plan involving an approved scheme of arrangement, the terms of which may not be agreeable to some shareholders, is binding on all shareholders, despite having an express provision requiring an exit option to dissenting shareholders.

---

[19] Greenhalgh v. Arderne Cinemas Ltd., (No 2) [1946] 1 All ER 512; [1951] Ch 286.

[20] Mrs. Rashmi Seth v. Chemin (India) Pvt. Ltd., (1995) 82 Comp Cas 563 (CLB).

[21] Sandvik Asia Limited v. Bharat Kumar Padamsi and Ors., (2010) 2 CompLJ 255 (Bom).

[22] The Companies Bill, 2011: 57th Report, 75 (see n. 17).

C) Shareholders vis-a-vis Creditors

With the dispensing of the requirement of shareholders' approval, it becomes imperative to analyse the effect of the disparity that is now created by virtue of this deemed consent. As stated above, the CoC, being the approving authority of the Plan under section 30(4) of the IBC, consists of all the financial creditors of the debtor company; this means that, effectively, only the financial creditors consider the viability of a Plan. From a company law jurisprudence standpoint, however, an approval of shareholders, creditors and debenture-holders of the company is required to be obtained with a three-fourth majority of voters.[23] Due to the overriding effect of the IBC,[24] therefore, financial creditors (not all creditors) have the authority over the Plan. This results in disparity not only between shareholders and creditors, as creditors are placed at a higher pedestal, but also between the different kinds of creditors as the IBC allows only the financial creditors to form the CoC. Other types of creditors, such as operational creditors and other creditors who may not fall within the strict definition of "financial" or "operational" creditors, are excluded from voting on a Plan containing a scheme of arrangement. Accordingly, where the Companies Act requires a meeting of all creditors or each class of creditors or all members or each class of members for the purpose of voting on the scheme, this requirement has been diluted by a conjoint reading of sections 21(2), 31(1) and 238 of the IBC.

IV. International Scenario

After observing the position in India, reference should be made to the position of other jurisdictions regarding the above topics in order to gain a holistic perspective on the need and possibility of further developing the IBC with respect to the above-mentioned situations. As stated above, the BLRC had primarily referred to the insolvency and bankruptcy law of the United Kingdom and the United States; therefore, for the purpose of this paper as well, the relevant laws of these two jurisdictions have been taken into account.

In the Insolvency Act, 1986[25] of the UK, section 110, which provides for an arrangement of the company for which the liquidator has been appointed, enables the liquidator to transfer a business undertaking to

---

[23] The Companies Act of 2013, section 230(6).

[24] IBC, section 238.

[25] The Insolvency Act of 1986, United Kingdom, Chapter 45, http://www.legislation.gov.uk/ukpga/1986/45/pdfs/ukpga_19860045_en.pdf.

another company in exchange for new shares to the existing shareholders. Under this section, a shareholders' special resolution is required before such reconstruction/arrangement is implemented.[26] As discussed in the preceding paragraphs, when there is a proposed arrangement involving the transfer of shares or other assets of a company, and when there is a motion for such an arrangement, there may be some shareholders who vote against this resolution. Unlike the Indian IBC, the UK Insolvency Act accounts for such dissenting shareholders by enabling them to sell their shares to the official and exit the company.[27]

Providing for a more inclusive process, the United States Bankruptcy Code (US Code) provides for approval of each class of claims or interests. Section 1129 of the US Code, which provides for a "confirmation of plan", creates a mandate on the part of the court to determine, *inter alia,* that:

> (7) With respect to each *impaired class of claims or interests—*
> (A) *each holder of a claim or interest of such class—*
> (i) *has accepted the plan*; or
> (ii) *will receive or retain under the plan on account of such claim or interest property of a value, as of the effective date of the plan, that is not less than the amount that such holder would so receive or retain if the debtor were liquidated under chapter 7 of this title on such date*; or
>
> (B) if section 1111(b)(2) of this title applies to the claims of such class, each holder of a claim of such class will receive or retain under the plan on account of such claim property of a value, as of the effective date of the plan, that is not less than the value of such holder's interest in the estate's interest in the property that secures such claims.
> (8) With respect to *each class of claims or interests—*
> (A) such class has accepted the plan; or
> (B) such class is not impaired under the plan.

Moreover, the judicial approach with respect to the importance of shareholders' approval has been quite active in order to secure the interests of all stakeholders, including stockholders. In the case of *Esopus Creek Value LP v. Hauf,*[28] the Court of Chancery of Delaware observed that:

> To circumvent this apparent dead end, the board of directors adopted a plan to file a bankruptcy petition once the asset sale agreement [was] signed,

[26] UK Insolvency Act, 1986, section 110(3).
[27] UK Insolvency Act, 1986, section 111.
[28] Esopus Creek Value LP v. Hauf, 2006 WL 3499526 (Del. Ch. Nov. 29, 2006), http://caselaw.findlaw.com/de-court-of-chancery/1250206.html#footnote_3.

and thereafter seek approval of the sale from the bankruptcy court, without a meeting and without a vote by the common stockholders.

With reference to the above-quoted observation, it was also observed by the court that:

> The plan proposed further disadvantages the common stockholders because, in the bankruptcy proceeding, as proposed, the consent of two-thirds of the corporation's preferred stockholders is required in connection with the sale; whereas, outside of bankruptcy, the preferred stockholders have no vote on the transaction. The record reflects that the preferred stockholders have used this added leverage to negotiate advantageous terms for themselves in the proposed bankruptcy proceeding.

In the aforementioned case, the court had ordered against the management laying down the importance of shareholders' participation in any action involving their interest. Moreover, this principle can also be found in section 1126 of the US Code dealing with acceptance of a plan, which requires that:

> (d) A class of interests has accepted a plan if such plan has been accepted by holders of such interests, other than any entity designated under subsection (e) of this section, that hold at least two-thirds in amount of the allowed interests of such class held by holders of such interests, other than any entity designated under subsection (e) of this section, that have accepted or rejected such plan.

Further, the Senate Report No. 95-989 on this provision has observed that:

> Solicitations with respect to a plan do not involve just mere requests for opinions. Acceptance of the plan vitally affects creditors and shareholders, and most frequently the solicitation involves an offering of securities in exchange for claims or interests. […] Under subsection (d),[29] with respect to a class of equity securities, it is sufficient for acceptance of the plan if the amount of securities voting for the plan is at least two-thirds of the total actually voted.[30]

---

[29] Referring to section 1126(d) of the US Code.

[30] Senate Report No. 95-989, Office of the Law Revision Counsel, http://uscode.house.gov/view.xhtml;jsessionid=D88937393BD67CD9D6A48A0BABA79A34?path=&req=10+USC&f=treesort&fq=true&num=5660&hl=true&edition=prelim.

To conclude, despite the IBC being based on the experience of the UK Insolvency Act and the US Code, it fails to address various situations highlighted hereinabove, which the two laws of the respective jurisdictions do. Creating a disparity between shareholders and creditors, or not taking into account the concerns of shareholders in a resolution plan which may have adverse effects on their security holdings is not only inequitable, as already highlighted, but also a backward step in the development of the corporatisation era.

V. Conclusion and Suggestions

The objective of overhauling and simplifying the insolvency regime as part of the Central Government's initiative to attract foreign investment and to increase the ease of doing business by enactment of the IBC has not been able to achieve what it could have had there been more deliberation on the implementation scheme of the new law. Moreover, the government had the opportunity to address such concerns as have been raised by various stakeholders, but that was not done by the recently promulgated Insolvency and Bankruptcy Code (Amendment) Ordinance, 2017.[31]It will therefore be appropriate if we term it a "missed opportunity".

Where the judiciary is active in filling the lacunae that have arisen time and again, the Parliament has not addressed various issues satisfactorily. Where the issue of adherence to the principles of natural justice came up, as section 7 of the IBC did not provide for any opportunity of hearing, the judicial approach has been successful in addressing the hardship.[32] Another major development brought about by the judiciary has been in *Mobilox Innovations Private Limited v. Kirusa Software Private Limited,*[33] wherein, in order to uphold the intention of the IBC, the Hon'ble Supreme Court gave its authoritative interpretation on the word "and" appearing in section 8(2)(a) of the IBC so as to give to the provision relating to "dispute" its intended effect. Apart from such instances, there have been numerous other cases which have led to the development of the new law.

Before concluding this paper, it will be appropriate to address the major anomaly with regard to the rights of the shareholders in case of a Plan involving a scheme of arrangement by giving a suggestion as to the

[31] The Insolvency and Bankruptcy Code (Amendment) Ordinance of 2017, No. 7 of 2017, http://ibbi.gov.in/180404.pdf.

[32] Sree Metaliks Limited & Anr. v. Union of India, (W.P. 7144 (W) of 2017).

[33] Civil Appeal No. 9405 of 2017, judgement delivered by R.F. Nariman, J., http://supremecourtofindia.nic.in/supremecourt/2017/20386/20386_2017_Judgement_21-Sep-2017.pdf.

drafting of a provision which attempts to address the interests of such stakeholders as well. It is submitted that under subsection 2 of section 30—providing for the requirements of a Plan—a clause may be added to the following effect:

> (g) proposing a scheme of arrangement of the Corporate Debtor has received the consent of the majority as required by the Companies Act, 2013 and the rules made thereunder.

Further, after section 31(1), the following proviso may be inserted:

> Provided that, in case the resolution plan involves a scheme of arrangement or any action for which the Companies Act, 2013 requires a special resolution, the Adjudicating Authority shall, notwithstanding anything contained in this Code, ensure that the relevant provisions of the Act and the rules made thereunder have been complied with.

The above-mentioned suggested proviso caters not only to the situation of a Plan involving a scheme of restructuring or arrangement but also to any situation for which the Companies Act mandates a special resolution. This is because such situations are extra-ordinary, and in order to serve the interests of shareholders in such crucial circumstances, if not in ordinary functioning, a larger threshold is provided.

As the provisions of the IBC stand, the judicial approach will play, as has always been the case, a crucial role in the evolution of the principles which have been enshrined in the IBC but could not be crystallised. The purpose of this paper has been to highlight certain practical circumstances which, if addressed, would bring two important legislations—the Companies Act and the IBC—in consonance and parity with each other. Perhaps, similar to the Supreme Court's primer on the IBC in *M/s Innoventive Industries Ltd. v. ICICI Bank & Anr.*,[34] there will be a liberal interpretation to certain seemingly rigid provisions of the IBC in order to harmonise the corporate regime as a whole.

---

[34] Civil Appeal Nos. 8337-8338 of 2017, http://supremecourtofindia.nic.in/supremecourt/2017/17291/17291_2017_Judgement_31-Aug-2017.pdf.

CHAPTER III

FINANCING AN M&A TRANSACTION: THE BOND WAY TO DO IT

SAUMYA RAIZADA AND SWATI SHALINI

Abstract

In order to ensure that a mergers and acquisitions (M&A) transaction is completed effectively, it is important to find out an appropriate source of funding it. There are various sources available in the market to finance such a transaction; however, the objectives of the transaction and the financial status of the company concerned play a vital role in determining which type of source should be preferred. Bonds are one of the instruments which help in financing M&A transactions, and they are slowly and steadily picking up in India. Among the different types of bonds that a potential investor may utilise are normal bonds, rupee-denominated masala bonds and junk bonds. In this paper, the authors endeavour to briefly lead the reader on to understanding, through the first part, the importance of debt financing and how an M&A transaction can be funded by debt. In the second part of the paper, the relationship between bonds and M&A activities is discussed to examine why a company would be interested in financing such activities by issuing bonds. The third part deals with the various bond options available in the market and how they are regulated. Also included are sub-sections dealing with junk bonds and the case of a leveraged buyout in a country like India. The fourth part deals with debt refinancing following a corporate reconstruction activity. In the final part of the paper, the authors discuss the impact of credit ratings on M&A activities, the link between investor confidence and credit ratings, and the aptness of these agencies in the light of certain recent developments such as the proposed BRICS Credit Ratings Agency. The concluding remarks provide a brief insight into the future of such issuances.

Introduction

Financing is the act of providing funds for business activities, making purchases or investing.[1]The decision to finance involves making a choice between cash, debt and equity financing. Economies are usually composed of banks, investors and a target, with the acquirer having to choose between equity and debt, a bank loan or public traded bonds, to raise outside funds to cover the M&A transaction.[2] In this paper, the authors analyse the corporate bond market and examine the several options available in the form of masala bonds, green bonds and junk bonds to corporates seeking to fund an M&A transaction. A well-developed corporate bond market ensures that funds flow towards productive investments and market forces exert competitive pressures on lending to the private sector. While India boasts of a world-class equity market, its bond market is still relatively underdeveloped and is dominated by government bonds,[3] though a recent diversification of sorts has occurred and an increasing shift from banks to Non-Banking Financial Companies has been witnessed.[4]

Part I: Importance of Debt Financing—Lessons from the Asian Financial Crisis

Companies may issue bonds to finance their M&A operations. Most companies can borrow from banks, but they consider direct borrowing from a bank as more restrictive and expensive than selling debt in the open market by way of a bond issue.[5] This is when debt financing options and the ease thereof step in. A liquid corporate debt market can play a crucial role by supplementing the banking system to meet the requirements of the

---

[1] "Financing", Investopedia, accessed October 13, 2017, http://www.investopedia.com/terms/f/financing.asp.

[2] Fatma Hamza, "Choice between Bank Loans, Publicly Traded Debt and Equity in Mergers and Acquisitions," International Conference on Finance and Banking, accessed October 15, 2017, http://icfb.rs.opf.slu.cz/sites/icfb.rs.opf.slu.cz/files/12_hamza.pdf.

[3] Sunder Raghavan, Ashok Sahoo, Angshuman Hait, and Saurabh Ghosh, "A Study of Corporate Bond Market in India: Theoretical and Policy Implications", March 4, 2014, https://rbi.org.in/scripts/PublicationsView.aspx?id=15725.

[4] Hereinafter, NBFCs.

[5] Niklolas Lioudis, "Why do Companies issue debts and bonds? Can't they just borrow from the Banks?" Investopedia, accessed October 13, 2017, http://www.investopedia.com/ask/answers/05/reasonforcorporatebonds.asp.

corporate sector for long-term capital investment and asset creation.[6] An economy carries huge risks with an underdeveloped debt financing market and overdependence on banks to finance their projects. The Asian Financial Crisis is a lesson from the pages of history which should not be forgotten when it comes to debt financing options.

The Asian Financial Crisis of 1997 (also known as the "Asian Contagion") affected the economies of Thailand (where it began), Indonesia, South Korea, Malaysia, Singapore and the Philippines. Growth in the region's export economies led to high levels of foreign direct investment, which in turn led to soaring real estate values, bolder corporate spending and even large public infrastructure projects, all funded largely by heavy borrowing from banks.[7] It was a series of currency devaluations starting in Thailand and later spreading to other Asian countries due to the decision of the Thai local government to no longer peg the local currency to the US dollar. Currency declines spread rapidly throughout South Asia, in turn causing stock market declines, reduced import revenues and government upheaval.[8] The International Monetary Fund had to step in and provide emergency funds to help in the situation. This crisis can be seen as a lesson as to why overdependency on the banking system alone can cause turmoil for the whole economy, and it is therefore heartening to see that the RBI is encouraging debt financing, including issuance of bonds, for institutions other than banking companies. Speaking of bond markets specifically, the US bond market is comparatively more successful than the Indian bond market because of the continued issuing of high-yield bonds (which are bonds rated BB and below). The US market recognises the attractive risk-return characteristics of high-yield bonds, which enable high-growth companies to obtain financing. Besides investment grade, another credible success factor has been the maturity length of bonds.[9] The average maturity in the US bond

---

[6] Payal Ghose and N. Aparna Raja, "The Changing Dynamics of Debt Financing in India," CCIL Monthly Newsletter, May 2016, https://www.ccilindia.com/Documents/Rakshitra/2016/May/Article.pdf.

[7] Justin Kuepper, "What was the Asian Financial Crisis?" The Balance, accessed March 20, 2017, https://www.thebalance.com/what-was-the-asian-financial-crisis-1978997.

[8] "Asian Financial Crisis," Investopedia, accessed November 7, 2017, http://www.investopedia.com/terms/a/asian-financial-crisis.asp#ixzz4xaE25iW0.

[9] Kanad Chaudhari, Meenal Raje, and Charan Singh, "Corporate Bond Markets in India: A Study and Policy Recommendations," IIM Bangalore Working Papers Series: 450, February 2014, https://iimb.ac.in/research/sites/default/files/WP%20No.%20450.pdf.

market has lengthened in the recent past and has been upwards of 12 years since 2007.[10] Additionally, ultra-long-term bonds of maturities ranging from 30 to 50 years are also widely used.[11] These are typically useful investment avenues for long-term investors such as pension funds.[12]

Part II: Bonds and the M&A Scene

According to section 2(30) of the Companies Act, 2013, debenture includes debenture stock, bonds or any other instrument of a company showing a debt, whether constituting a charge on the assets of the company or not. Bonds are financial instruments used by corporations to raise capital. Corporate bonds are fixed-income securities issued by corporates (i.e., entities other than the government).[13] They are a kind of loan agreement in which the investors pay money by buying corporate bond in a company, and the company has an obligation to pay interest on the principal amount and the whole amount when the bond matures. Bonds carry their own set of risks such as credit or default risk, call risk and inflation risk. The risks carried by bonds can be assessed by a credit rating agency, which usually finds out the ability of a company to pay off its debt and helps the investors to evaluate the associated risks and determine the interest rate payable on the principal.[14]

With banks unwilling to lower their base rates, the corporate bond market has picked itself up and has established itself as an easy alternative to bank credit. While RBI slashed the liquidity adjustment facility repo rate by 50 bps between December 2014 and March 2015, for example, the banks' inability to replicate this change led corporates to tap the bond market, as is evident from the higher number of issuances (2,371 in 2014–15) and lower average fixed rate coupon (from 11.34% in 2012–13 to 11.09 in 2014–15%).[15]

---

[10] Kanad Chaudhari, 8.

[11] Kanad Chaudhari, 8.

[12] Kanad Chaudhari, 8.

[13] "FAQ on Corporate Bond," National Stock Exchange of India Limited, September 29, 2011, https://www.nseindia.com/products/content/debt/corp_bonds/FAQ_corporate_bond.pdf.

[14] "What are Corporate Bonds?" Investor Bulletin, U.S. Securities and Exchange Commission Office of Investor Education and Advocacy, SEC Pub. No. 149 (6/13),accessed November 11, 2017, https://www.sec.gov/investor/alerts/ib_corporatebonds.pdf.

[15]"What are Corporate Bonds?" 5.

Looking at the RBI's Financial Stability Report, 2017, it is easy to see that during 2016–17, while deposit growth of scheduled commercial banks (SCBs) picked up, credit growth remained sluggish, putting pressure on net interest income (NII), particularly of the public-sector banks (PSBs).[16] This report highlights a rare phenomenon where banks' credit to the commercial sector dropped below the 50% mark.[17] The fall may be interpreted as the collapse of economic activity, but the aggregate credit of banks through bonds rose 24.3% last fiscal, reflecting continued robust credit supply.[18]Although Indian banks may be struggling to lend money to corporates, this does not imply that the M&A scene in India has gone for a toss. This is further evident from the fact that the M&A activity involving Indian companies during the quarter January–March 2017 stood at 252 deals with a total disclosed value of $15.8 billion, up from $12.8 billion in the corresponding period last year.[19] With the Indian banks becoming less competitive, the Indian masala bond has emerged as a shining star, with many companies and firms tapping it to finance their projects and expand their reach.

Part III: Selecting the Most Viable Bond from the Options in the Market

As stated above, companies have various bond options available to finance their transactions depending upon the purpose thereof. An Indian company transacting with a foreign company may issue offshore bonds for the reasons addressed later in this sub-section of the paper. Issuing masala bonds for offshore funding is more effective in that the debt securities issued outside India in the form of Indian currency help the Indian firms to raise capital. Another type of bond, popularly referred to as "the green bond", is available for firms engaged in green projects. The

---

[16] *Financial Stability Report June 2017*, Reserve Bank of India, June 30, 2017, https://rbi.org.in/Scripts/PublicationReportDetails.aspx?UrlPage=&ID=876.
[17] Saloni Shukla, "Top Corporates are moving away from banks as MFs & insurers throw cheaper funds", *The Economic Times*, July12, 2017, http://economictimes.indiatimes.com/industry/banking/finance/banking/banks-must-find-out-ways-to-protect-its-earnings-while-lifting-fee-income/articleshow/59551753.cms.
[18] Saloni Shukla. The Economic Times.
[19] T.E. Narasimhan, "Indian M&A deals up 23% to $16 bn in Jan-March even as volumes remain flat," *Business Standard*, May 24, 2017, http://www.business-standard.com/article/companies/indian-m-a-deals-rose-by-23-in-value-to-15-8-billion-in-q1-of-2017-117052301153_1.html.

tax structure of a green bond is also quite flexible. If the firms wish to issue a tax-free infrastructure bond, they can rely on green bonds to finance their green projects in renewable energy sectors. Likewise, junk bonds are issued by investors who wish to get high returns and are at the same time capable of sustaining high risks.

A) Offshore Bonds: Why Do Firms Issue Abroad?

Asia has the largest number of firms active in the offshore bond market (nearly 1,000), but the value of the debt issued by Latin American firms (US$639 billion) overshadows that of the debt issued by Asian ones (US$273 billion).[20] Most companies raise funds in foreign currency; only 14% have issued bonds in local currency.[21] An examination of the available data reveals that firms increasingly issue abroad due to myriad factors such as:

1. satiating the investor demands for a higher yield;
2. having a backup option when the onshore market has a crisis situation;
3. stability of the economy in the foreign country;
4. easier conditions of external financing as compared to those prevailing in the local country—this usually happens with the less-developed countries or the developing countries;
5. arbitraging price differentials, gaining access to foreign investors, or issuing larger, lower-rated or longer-maturity bonds.[22]

B) Preventing India from Committing the "Original Sin" of Economies: The Masala Bond

In the Indian scenario, the International Finance Corporation (IFC) launched the first masala bonds with the launch of the Rupee-Linked Offshore Bond programme in the year 2013. These bonds—internationally issued debt of Indian entities denominated in the Indian rupee—are often positioned as a panacea that will prevent India from committing the

[20] José María Serena and Ramon Moreno, "Domestic Financial Markets and Offshore bond financing," BIS Quarterly Review, September 2016, https://www.bis.org/publ/qtrpdf/r_qt1609g.htm.

[21] Serena, "Domestic Financial Markets and Offshore bond financing."

[22] Susan Black and Anella Munro, "Why issue bonds offshore?" BIS Working Papers No. 334, December 2010, http://www.bis.org/publ/work334.pdf.

"original sin" of economics.[23] This "original sin" refers to the inability to borrow abroad in terms of domestic currency, and borrowing domestically.[24] These offshore bonds, called masala bonds, are plain vanilla bonds that are issued by the Indian borrowers in offshore countries, where investors pay the foreign currency equivalent of the rupee principal amount at the time of issuance and at the time of payment of interest as well as redemption. They then receive the foreign currency equivalent of the rupee coupon/redemption amount due. The applicable foreign currency-rupee conversion rate is the market rate on the date of settlement of transactions undertaken for issue, interest payment and redemption.[25]

Masala bonds are similar to debt securities as defined under section 2(30) of the Companies Act, 2013. The provisions applicable to debentures are, therefore, applicable to masala bonds; however, when Indian companies issue masala bonds as part of the External Commercial Borrowings (ECB) policy framework of the RBI, they are not required to comply with the provisions of Chapter III of the Companies Act, 2013 and Rule 18 of the Companies (Share Capital and Debenture) Rules, 2014.[26]

In a recent circular dated April 13, 2016, the RBI has made certain changes to the guidelines for the issue of masala bonds. The highlights of the modifications are as follows:[27]

1. The minimum maturity period of masala bonds that are issued outside India has been reduced from five years to three years, making it similar with the maturity period of general corporate bonds.

[23] Deep Narayan, "Masala bonds are no silver lining," Livemint, September 13, 2016, http://www.livemint.com/Opinion/0DrRJqIi424nJKBV8KhtgO/Masala-bonds-are-no-silver-bullet.html.

[24] Michael D. Bordo, Christopher Meissner, and Angela Redish, "How 'Original Sin' was Overcome: The Evolution of External Debt Denominated in Domestic Currencies in the United States and the British Dominions," National Bureau of Economic Research Working Paper No. 9841, July 2003, http://www.nber.org/papers/w9841.

[25] Sargam Marwaha, "Masala Bonds—Unraveling the Secret Ingredients," Taxmann Online, [2017] 84 taxmann.com 35 (Article)/[2017] 143 SCL 19 (Article).

[26] General Circular No. 9/2016, Ministry of Corporate Affairs, August 3, 2016, http://www.mca.gov.in/Ministry/pdf/GeneralCircular09_03082016.pdf.

[27] "Issuance of Rupee denominated bonds overseas," A.P. (DIR Series) Circular No.60, Reserve Bank of India, April 13, 2016, https://www.rbi.org.in/Scripts/BS_CircularIndexDisplay.aspx?Id=10350.

2. The maximum amount which can be borrowed by the enterprises by issuing masala bonds is now Rs. 50 billion and not US$750 million as it was under the Masala Bond Guidelines.
3. Masala bonds can now be issued to:
   a. an entity that is a resident of a country which is a member of the Financial Action Task Force (FATF);
   b. the securities market regulator, which is a signatory to the International Organization of Securities Commissions' Multilateral Memorandum of Understanding;
   c. an entity that is a resident of a country which is FATF compliant.

Recent Issuances of Masala Bonds

In March 2016, the IFC launched an innovative masala bond to mobilise Japanese investment in India's private sector.[28] This provides a scope for Japanese household investors to participate in the Indian economy easily.[29] In the year 2016, it issued a 15-year masala bond. This bond created an offshore-rupee market that is stretched from three to 15years.[30] The London Stock Exchange welcomed the IFC to mark the listing of the masala bond, the longest-dated offshore-rupee bond ever issued. The bond raised Rs. 2 billion (or nearly $30 million), highlighting long-term investor confidence in India.[31] Recently, the RBI—via its circular dated September 22, 2017—to further harmonise the issuance of masala bonds in accordance with ECB guidelines, stated that, with effect from October 3, 2017, masala bonds will no longer form part of the limit for FPI Investments in corporate bonds. They will form part of ECBs and will be monitored accordingly.[32]

---

[28] Sargam Marwaha, "Masala Bonds—Unraveling the Secret Ingredients" (see n. 25).
[29] Sargam Marwaha, "Masala Bonds—Unraveling the Secret Ingredients" (see n. 25).
[30] "IFC in India," International Finance Corporation, World Bank Group https://www.ifc.org/wps/wcm/connect/dbf85c004c7809549365bbd4c83f5107/IFC+in+India_04April+2016.pdf?MOD=AJPERES.
[31] "London Stock Exchange Welcomes IFC," London Stock Exchange press release, accessed November 7, 2017, https://www.lseg.com/markets-products-and-services/our-markets/london-stock-exchange/equities-markets/raising-equity-finance/market-open-ceremony/london-stock-exchange-welcomes-ifc.
[32] "Investment by Foreign Portfolio Investors in Corporate Debt Securities – Review," A.P. (DIR Series) Circular No. 05, Reserve Bank of India, September 22, 2017, https://rbi.org.in/Scripts/NotificationUser.aspx?Id=11127&Mode=0.

Relaxation of Regulations Enjoyed by Offshore-rupee Bonds

Transactions due to ECBs and trade credits are governed by clause (d) of subsection 3 of section 6 of the Foreign Exchange Management Act, 1999 (FEMA).[33] Various provisions in respect of these two types of borrowings from overseas are included in the three regulations framed under FEMA, *viz.* the Foreign Exchange Management (Borrowing or Lending in Foreign Exchange) Regulations, 2000,[34] the Foreign Exchange Management (Transfer or Issue of any Foreign Security) Regulations, 2004,[35] and the Foreign Exchange Management (Guarantees) Regulations, 2000.[36]

These restrictions, however, have been done away with in relation to masala bonds, and, therefore, Indian corporates (including infrastructure investment trusts and real estate investment trusts) can proceed to raise funds outside India without having to follow such stringent requirements that are otherwise required of the ECBs.

Factors such as tax burden and liquidity remain a concern even after the government plans on welcoming issuers to take the masala bond route. In what can be seen as a setback for the M&A finance scenario, the government still charges a withholding tax on income from offshore-rupee bonds. The matter of taxation of offshore rupee-denominated bonds falls under the Income Tax Act, 1961. In the case of non-resident investors, the CBDT has clarified that during the taxation of interest income from these offshore-rupee bonds, withholding tax at the rate of 5%, would be

[33] "Master Direction—External Commercial Borrowings, Trade Credit, Borrowing and Lending in Foreign Currency by Authorised Dealers and Persons other than Authorised Dealers," FED Master Direction No.5/2015-16, Reserve Bank of India, last updated March 30, 2016, https://rbi.org.in/scripts/BS_ViewMasDirections.aspx?id=10204.

[34] Notified via Notification No. FEMA 3/2000-RB dated May 3, 2000, https://www.rbi.org.in/Scripts/NotificationUser.aspx?Id=157&Mode=0.

[35] "Foreign Exchange Management (Transfer or issue of security by a person resident outside India) Regulations, 2000," Notification No. FEMA 20 /2000-RB, Reserve Bank of India, May 3, 2000, https://rbi.org.in/scripts/BS_FemaNotifications.aspx?Id=174; "Foreign Exchange Management (Transfer or Issue of Any Foreign Security) (Amendment) Regulations, 2004," Notification No. FEMA 120/2004-RB, Reserve Bank of India, July 7, 2004, https://rbi.org.in/scripts/BS_FemaNotifications.aspx?Id=2126.

[36] Notified via Notification No. FEMA 8/2000-RB dated May 3, 2000, https://www.rbi.org.in/Scripts/NotificationUser.aspx?Id=162&Mode=0.

applicable in the same way as it is applicable for offshore dollar-denominated bonds.[37]

In what can be seen as a welcoming move, exemption from capital gains would be available in case it arises from appreciation of the rupee between the date of issue and the date of redemption against the foreign currency in which the investment is made.[38] Further, as indicated above, rupee-denominated bonds sold overseas will not form a part of the investment limit for the Foreign Portfolio Investors (FPIs) in corporate bonds and shall instead be a part of ECBs.[39] This will allow companies to issue masala bonds as they are currently barred by Securities and Exchange Board of India (SEBI), which previously came out with a notification stating that "Rupee denominated bonds issued by Indian corporates overseas are covered under CCDL, issuance of such bonds overseas shall temporarily cease, until the limit utilization falls back to below 92%."[40]

Green Bonds: A One-Step Solution to Financing Green Projects

A green bond is a type of general corporate bond which is issued by an entity to raise capital from the investors. The only difference between a green bond and a corporate bond is that the former is issued to finance green projects, assets or activities with environmental benefits.[41] The aim

---

[37] "Taxation of income from off-shore Rupee Denominated Bonds," Central Board of Direct Taxes press release, October 29, 2015, http://www.incometaxindia.gov.in/Lists/Press%20Releases/Attachments/404/Press-Release-Off-shore-Rupee-Denominated-Bonds-29-10-2015.pdf.

[38] Shripal Lakdawala, Dhawal Bhathawala, and Tejal Seta, "Clarity on Tax Implications in respect of Rupee Denominated Bonds," Taxmann, February 14, 2017, https://www.taxmann.com/budget-2017-18/budget/t109/clarity-on-tax-implications-in-respect-of-rupee-denominated-bonds.aspx.

[39] "Investment by Foreign Portfolio Investors in Corporate Debt Securities – Review," A.P. (DIR Series) Circular No. 05, Reserve Bank of India, September 22, 2017, https://rbidocs.rbi.org.in/rdocs/notification/PDFs/APDIR522091746D54E9902984BD593836C5064285D70.PDF.

[40] "Investments by FPIs in Corporate Debt," IMD/FPIC/CIR/P/2017/81, Securities and Exchange Board of India, July 20, 2017, http://www.sebi.gov.in/legal/circulars/jul-2017/investments-by-fpis-in-corporate-debt_35362.html.

[41] "Concept paper for issuance of Green Bonds," Securities and Exchange Board of India, December 3, 2015, http://www.sebi.gov.in/reports/reports/dec-2015/ concept-paper-for-issuance-of-green-bonds_31167.html.

of green bonds is to meet the environmental targets of the investors and the government. The renewable energy sector is evolving faster than expected. In 2014, renewable energy contributed half of the world's new power generation.[42] It is one of the largest sources of electricity. The Ministry of New and Renewable Energy, after considering the report of the Central Electricity Authority in the 18th Electric Power Survey with regard to demand for electricity by the year 2021–22, has set a target of achieving 175GW of renewable energy by 2022.[43] To achieve this target, a large amount of money is required to implement renewable energy projects. The introduction of green bonds is a vital step taken by SEBI to promote financing of green projects in India. Green bonds attract investors who wish to make a responsible investment.

Recent Issuances of Green Bonds in India

In the year 2015, India issued US$1.1 billion in green bonds.[44] Yes Bank issued India's first Euro-denominated green bond in February 2015,[45] followed by another issuance in August 2015. The latter issue was entirely financed by the IFC.[46]

The SEBI (Issue and Listing of Debt Securities) Regulations, 2008 govern public issue of debt securities and listing of debt securities.[47] Green

---

42 "Renewables," The IEA's 2015 World Energy Outlook (WEO), International Energy Agency, accessed November 18, 2017, https://www.iea.org/topics/renewables/.

43 No. 11/1/2016-EFM, Ministry of New and Renewable Energy, February 11, 2016, http://mnre.gov.in/file-manager/UserFiles/RPO-Targets-upto-2022.pdf.

44 "Greening India's Financial Market: How Green Bonds Can Drive Clean Energy Deployment," Natural Resources Defense Council (NRDC), April 2016, https://www.nrdc.org/sites/default/files/india-financial-market-green-bonds-report.pdf.

45 "Yes Bank successfully issues India's first green infrastructure bonds," Yes Bank press release, February 25, 2015, https://www.yesbank.in/media/press-releases/fy-2014-15/yes-bank-successfully-issues-india-s-first-green-infrastructure-bond.html.

46 "Yes Bank signs Green Finance Charter with European Development Finance Institutions – FMO of Netherlands, DEG of Germany and Proparco of France," Yes Bank press release, June 20, 2017, https://www.yesbank.in/media/press-releases/yes-bank-signs-green-finance-charter-with-european-development-finance-institutions-fmo-of-netherlands-deg-of-germany-and-proparco-of-france.

47 "Disclosure Requirements for Issuance and Listing Green Bonds," Securities and Exchange Board of India Memorandum to the Board, February 24, 2017,

bonds are issued in India under these regulations.[48] In the round-table discussion hosted by the Indian Renewable Energy Development Authority (IREDA), the Indian Ministry of New and Renewable Energy stated that green bonds currently fund, among other things, renewable energy (38.3%), building and industry (27.5%), transport (10.2%), water (9.7%), waste management (6.2%) and climate adaptation (4.3%).[49]

Generally, investors have the ability to invest in a project or enable the investment, but they lack the tools to make the investment happen. To solve this problem and to address climate-related concerns, the IFC has partnered with the leading asset management company Amundi to launch the world's largest green bond fund.[50]

The IFC's Introduction of Green Masala Bonds

The IFC issued a five-year green masala bond on the London Stock Exchange.[51] The issuing of this bond will help develop climate-friendly investments in India. The financing of M&A transactions in India for green projects will be easier; for instance, in February 2015, Singapore's Sembcorp Industries announced that it would acquire a 60% stake in Green Infra, a renewable energy company in India in the wind and solar sector.[52] Hyderabad-based renewable energy firm Greenko Group raised $1 billion through green bonds, the largest such issue so far in Asia. The company plans to use the funds to refinance $500 million in bonds issued in 2014 as well as for refinancing debt acquired through the 2016

---

http://www.sebi.gov.in/sebi_data/meetingfiles/feb-2017/1487934575665_1.pdf.

[48] "Greening India's Financial Market," NRDC (see n. 44).

[49] "Greening India's Financial Market," NRDC (see n. 44).

[50] "Green-Bond Fund Offers Green Path for Emerging Markets," International Finance Corporation press release, April 2017, http://www.ifc.org/wps/wcm/connect/news_ext_content/ifc_external_corporate_site/news+and+events/news/impact-stories/green-bond-fund-offers-green-path-for-emerging-markets.

[51] "IFC Issues First Green Masala Bond," International Finance Corporation press release, August 2015, http://www.ifc.org/wps/wcm/connect/news_ext_content/ifc_external_corporate_site/news+and+events/news/ifc+issues+first+green+masala+bond+on+london+stock+exchange.

[52] Narae Kim, "India's green issuers set to make a dash for cash," *Global Capital*, March 23, 2016, http://www.globalcapital.com/article/x1jfh4plghkx/indias-green-issuers-set-to-make-a-dash-for-cash.

acquisition of the now-bankrupt American renewable energy firm Sun Edison's solar assets in India.[53]

Funding Problems in India—A Case for Leveraged Buyouts and Junk Bonds

In India, financing an M&A transaction is not a cakewalk. Companies have to comply with several restrictions to fund their M&A transactions, which therefore makes leveraged buyout a distant dream for the companies.

Understanding the Concept of Leveraged Buyout

A leveraged buyout (LBO) is the acquisition of another company using a significant amount of borrowed money to meet the cost of acquisition. The assets of the company being acquired are often used as collateral for the loans, along with the assets of the acquiring company.[54]

A very recent LBO transaction has been the acquisition by Nirma, a detergent manufacturer, of Lafarge Cements. Nirma decided to raise approximately Rs. 4,000–4,500 crore via corporate bonds to fund the acquisition and used Lafarge's cash flow to repay it. Nirma had limited options for funding the acquisition, since banks are not allowed to lend money to a company that is buying 100% of the equity in another company. Nirma could have raised equity, borrowed from a non-bank lender or issued bonds through a special purpose vehicle. The bond market proved to be the cheapest option, offering a coupon 250 bps lower than a loan from an NBFC. The yields on AA-rated five-year corporate bonds are hovering around 7.98%.[55]

---

[53] Swaraj Singh Dhanjal, "Essel Group may raise $1 billion to refinance offshore debt," *Livemint*, July 27, 2017, http://www.livemint.com/Companies/kCuEyZsKKLRcBMRnt2giqK/Essel-Group-may-raise-1-billion-to-refinance-offshore-debt.html.

[54] "Leveraged Buyout – LBO," Investopedia, accessed October 10, 2017, https://www.investopedia.com/terms/l/leveragedbuyout.asp.

[55] "Nirma cements India's biggest M&A bond," *The Hindu Business Line*, September 19, 2016 http://www.thehindubusinessline.com/markets/nirma-cements-indias-biggest-ma-bond/article9123699.ece.

A Case for Utilising Junk Bonds

Junk bonds are corporate bonds that have the potential to have a higher return as compared to the others. These bonds are also known as high-yield bonds; however, these bonds also have a higher default risk. Moody's Investor Service has rated this kind of bond "BA or below".[56] They are therefore also known as "non-investment grade bonds". A bond bearing a rating below the minimum investment grade, which is BBB-, is considered a high-yield bond as it carries a higher risk. The investors who are willing to take high risks issue junk bonds. If the on-going business condition of the company is good, the investors get a high return. The junk bonds have a high return to compensate for the high risks involved in them. From an investor's perspective, junk bonds help to provide income and potential capital gains.

In India, during the beginning of the year 2017, total issuances of junk bonds were nearly 15 times higher than the money raised in the last year.[57] In May 2013, Rolta India Ltd. raised $200 million in an overseas bond carrying BB- ratings from S&P and Fitch.[58] The issue of this bond attracted over 200 investors.

In the year 2016, low-rated Indian companies raised about $5billion overseas.[59] Delhi International Airport, Jubilant Pharma, Novelis and Indiabulls Housing Finance collectively issued bonds worth $4.873 billion.[60] During the January–April 2017 period, the companies which were rated below the investment grade sold bonds worth $2.982 billion

---

[56] "What's in a Rating? The Meaning of Bond Ratings," Article by Wealth Management Systems, Inc. courtesy of a Morgan Stanley Financial Advisor, Morgan Stanley, accessed October 13, 2017, http://www.morganstanleyfa.com/public/projectfiles/c1d77225-96fc-40c5-a775-b331e0106041.pdf.

[57] Saikat Das, "How junk bonds are catching investor fancy," *The Economic Times*, April 27, 2017, https://economictimes.indiatimes.com/markets/bonds/how-junk-bonds-are-catching-investor-fancy/articleshow/58403471.cms.

[58] Dinesh Unnikrishnan, "Are junk bonds gaining ground in India," *Livemint*, last modified May 20, 2014, http://www.livemint.com/Money/BxzvsvOd3QRJor6GLahodO/Are-junk-bonds-gaining-ground-in-India.html.

[59] Saikat Das, "India Inc attracting global investors with high-yield bonds," *The Economic Times*, last updated October 26, 2016, https://economictimes.indiatimes.com/markets/bonds/indiainc-attracting-global-investors-with-high-yieldbonds/articleshow/55071831.cms.

[60] "What's in a Rating?" Morgan Stanley (see n. 56).

compared with $201.27 million in the same period last year.[61] The US junk bond market, during the period 2009–2015, rose 80% to $1.3 trillion.[62] Junk bonds and stock go hand in hand. If the stock market is doing well, it is presumed that the high yield will also do well. In the US, State Street Global Advisor's flagship junk bond fund is the SPDR Bloomberg Barclays High Yield Bond ETF, with more than $12 billion in assets. The bond has a yield of around 5% based on the last 30 days of distributions. It holds 905 bonds in the portfolio. The fund has an expense ratio of 0.45% or $40 per $10,000 invested.[63]

The main advantage of issuing junk bonds is that it offers higher yields compared to the investment grade bond. Junk bonds offer a larger maturity period compared to other types of financing. Moreover, this bond is a less costly source of funding than the other sources.[64] Initially, when the junk bond was introduced, it was used mostly for financing M&A transactions. Now, it is also used for other corporate purposes; however, the main disadvantage of using junk bonds is that if the business defaults the investor will lose 100% of his/her initial investment.[65]

Part IV: M&A and Debt Refinancing

Sometimes, firms may want to refinance a debt for reasons like lower interest rates and abundance of liquidity in the markets. The offshore refinancing market has seen significant activity in the last two years, and several Indian companies have tapped the opportunity provided by low interest rates, high liquidity and improving domestic macroeconomic factors to refinance debt.[66]

Saint-Gobain can be cited as the leading example of a case where post-acquisition recovery took place because of refinancing. Euro bonds were

---

[61]"What's in a Rating?" Morgan Stanley (see n. 56).

[62] Kimberly Amadeo, "Junk Bonds, Pros, Cons, and Ratings: Why Would a Person Invest in Junk Bonds?" *The Balance*, last updated May 21, 2018, https://www.thebalance.com/what-are-junk-bonds-pros-cons-ratings-3305606.

[63] Jeff Reeves, "Why Investors Seek Junk Bonds," *U.S. News*, September 28, 2017, https://money.usnews.com/investing/bonds/articles/2017-09-28/why-investors-seek-junk-bonds.

[64] Martin S. Fridson, "Junk Bonds," Encyclopedia of Business, 2nd ed., http://www.referenceforbusiness.com/encyclopedia/Int-Jun/Junk-Bonds.html.

[65] Saikat Das, "India Inc attracting global investors with high-yield bonds," (see n. 59).

[66] Swaraj Singh Dhanjal, "Essel Group may raise $1 billion to refinance offshore debt," (see n. 53).

issued by Saint-Gobain to refinance bank debt backing its purchase of Britain's BPB plc and to fund general corporate purposes. Another renewable energy firm, ReNew Power Ventures Pvt. Ltd., raised around $50 million in debt from Yes Bank Ltd. to refinance the debt of one of its wind power projects.[67] In January, Vedanta Resources plc raised $1 billion by selling bonds to refinance its near-term debt obligations. Vedanta bought back two series of bonds maturing in 2018 and 2019 worth a total of around $800 million.[68]Less than a year after its last offering, India's leading clean energy company, Greenko, is raising up to $1.1billion via an offshore dollar issue—the largest green bond sale to date by a company in Asia. Proceeds will be used to refinance the company's first dollar bond sale, which fetched $500 million in 2014. Additionally, the sale will also help the company refinance the debt that it inherited along with the acquisition of the 350 MW India portfolio of the bankrupt Sun Edison last year.[69] Looking at the above examples, it is quite evident that refinancing debt following corporate reconstruction processes is just as lucrative as financing the same through bonds.

Part V: Impact of Credit Ratings on M&A Activity

When bonds are issued, a credit rating is usually assigned to them by a credit rating agency. Three of the major agencies are Standard & Poor's, Moody's and Fitch, which charge issuers to rate their debts and financial instruments. These ratings incorporate a variety of factors, including the strength of the issuer's finances and its future prospects, and they allow investors to gain a sense of how likely a bond is to default

---

[67] Swaraj Singh Dhanjal, "ReNew Power Ventures raises $50 million in debt from Yes Bank," *Livemint*, August 18, 2017, http://www.livemint.com/Companies/9PZbubGFGCQpaO1FTwBEgM/ReNew-Power-Ventures-raises-50-mn-in-debt-from-Yes-Bank.html.

[68] Deborshi Chaki and Swaraj Singh Dhanjal, "Vedanta Resources raises $1billion via bond sale to refinance near-term debt," *Livemint*, January 26, 2017, http://www.livemint.com/Companies/vscMUFai4JYDRyOph3WScI/Vedanta-Resources-raises-1-billion-via-bond-sale-to-refinan.html.

[69] Arijit Barman and Saikat Das, "Greenko to raise $1 billion via Asia's largest green bond," *The Economic Times*, July 11, 2017, https://economictimes.indiatimes.com/markets/stocks/news/greenko-to-raise-950-million-green-bond-largest-in-asia/articleshow/59521936.cms.

(or, in other words, fail to make its interest and principal payments on time).[70]

AAA and AA are the two highest credit ratings with respect to bonds. Higher-quality bonds tend to perform better than lower-quality securities, even during times of economic distress, since the underlying issuers have sufficient financial strength to keep making their payments even under adverse conditions.[71]

Impact of Credit Ratings on Investor Confidence

Bond ratings are important not only for their role in informing investors but also because they affect the interest rate that companies and government agencies pay on their issued bonds.[72] International ratings play an important role for governments and companies in emerging countries like India in enabling them to raise capital in the international financial market.[73] It thus becomes important for India to perform better to get better credit ratings and/or go forward with an independent agency such as the BRICS Credit Rating Agency because better ratings would definitely mean more foreign investment in India.

A company with a good balance sheet and fair business prospect will enjoy a high credit rating.[74] Such a company will offer a competitive rate of interest but need not go out of the way to attract investors in its bonds or deposits.[75] A company with an AA rating, however, will surely offer more rate of interest than a company with an AAA rating.[76] In what can be seen as a positive step, Moody's has upgraded the credit rating of India Sovereign from Baa2 to Baa3 and changed the outlook on the ratings from

---

[70] Thomas Kenny, "Bond Credit Ratings," *The Balance*, last updated April 18, 2018, https://www.thebalance.com/what-are-bond-credit-ratings-417074.

[71] Swaraj Singh Dhanjal, "ReNew Power Ventures raises $50 million in debt from Yes Bank," (see n. 67).

[72] "Bond Rating Agencies," Investopedia, October 12, 2017, http://www.investopedia.com/terms/b/bond-rating-agencies.asp.

[73] Pravakar Sahoo and Bhavesh Garg, "India's current credit rating does not reflect the stability of the economy", *Hindustan Times*, last modified May 25, 2017, http://www.hindustantimes.com/opinion/india-s-current-credit-rating-does-not-reflect-the-stability-of-the-economy/story-8diQergcOmnN8fWKZWk6GL.html.

[74] "How does a change in credit rating impact your bond investments?" *Moneycontrol*, September 26, 2017, http://www.moneycontrol.com/news/business/personal-finance-business/how-does-a-change-in-credit-rating-impact-your-bond-investments-2397645.html.

[75] "How does a change in credit rating impact your bond investments?" *Moneycontrol*.

[76] "How does a change in credit rating impact your bond investments?" *Moneycontrol*.

"positive" to "stable" on October 2, 2017.[77] Moody's also upgraded the issuer ratings of nine state-owned firms, including oil producer Oil and Natural Gas Corp. (ONGC), refiners Indian Oil Corp. (IOC), Bharat Petroleum Corp. Ltd (BPCL) and Hindustan Petroleum Corp. Ltd (HPCL), power generator NTPC and gas utility GAIL (India). This could be the result of the labour put in by India in assuring returns to investors.

Analysing the Suitability of Credit Rating Agencies

The credit rating agencies have often rated the US better than countries like India. Critics have time and again slammed these agencies for being biased; for instance, they argue that India's credit rating has not become better in proportion to its growth and still remains just a notch above the "speculative grade" category. Lack of accountability towards market participants is another issue when it comes to such rating agencies. The agencies have enormous power in the market as they are used by sovereigns worldwide for the primary assessment of creditworthiness,[78] and concerns have been raised as regards the manner in which such power is used. Speaking at the BRICS Financial Forum organised by EXIM bank in Goa, alongside the BRICS leaders' meet, K. V. Kamath, President of the New Development Bank, backed the idea of creating an independent BRICS credit rating agency.[79] How and to what extent the plan would actually be put to use is something only time will tell.

Conclusion

A well-developed corporate bond market is the need of the hour for a developing country like India. With the RBI encouraging corporates to borrow from sources other than traditional banks and relaxing its grip on the offshore masala bonds, it looks to be a pleasant ride for the investors

---

[77] "Moody's upgrade Sovereign Credit Rating of India to Baa2 from Baa3," Press Information Bureau, Government of India, Ministry of Finance, November 17, 2017, http://pib.nic.in/newsite/PrintRelease.aspx?relid=173609.

[78] Preety Bhogal, "Rethinking the relevance of existing credit rating agencies to BRICS," Observer Research Foundation Occasional Papers, May 8, 2017, http://www.orfonline.org/research/rethinking-the-relevance-of-existing-credit-rating-agencies-to-brics/.

[79] Alexandra Katz, "BRICS in Search of business model for new rating agency," Russia Beyond, October 18, 2016, https://www.rbth.com/economics/finance/2016/10/18/brics-in-search-of-business-model-for-new-rating-agency_639889.

seeking to undertake M&A activity in India; however, in order to keep pace with the international bond market, the RBI shall have to be more regular with its efforts to encourage corporates to finance their transactions through bonds. Steps to make the bond market developed enough to ensure that the issuance costs decline, that liquidity and trading pick up and that firms issue more bonds will be needed now more than ever with the corporate bond market responding positively to both masala bonds and green bonds (including green masala bonds). Firms which are well set and can risk some investment have started considering the issuance of junk bonds in India after successful junk bonds issuances in the West. As the junk bond picks up in the market, the high return at the end of the bond issuance will only lead to better M&A prospects for the country. Investors, however, look at the credit rating of the corporate issuing the bond due to the inherent risks associated therewith. This is a cause of concern for Indian companies, with the three premier credit ratings being harsh on them with their ratings. Although Moody's has recently revised its ratings in the favour of India Sovereign, this is not enough to compete with other developing nations like China. An alternative in the form of a BRICS Credit Rating Agency is proposed, the implementation and success of which remains to be seen.

CHAPTER IV

ANTITRUST TRENDS IN E-COMMERCE MERGERS AND ACQUISITIONS

RHEA SINGH AND VARSHINI RAMESH

Abstract

The merger mania being witnessed for quite some time now is a sign of the disappearance of competition. This article questions the capability of traditional competition laws to effectively keep up with the dynamic nature of high-technology markets. With increased consolidations taking place in this field, a remodelled definition of the "relevant market" is warranted. More specifically, this article deals with horizontal mergers, which are notorious for raising anti-competitive concerns. Matured markets face the wrath of monopolists, which is why careful scrutiny by anti-trust regulators is encouraged; however, markets must be allowed to freely compete so that network effects pick the business model that provides maximum consumer welfare. The article focuses primarily on the e-retail and the cab aggregator sectors of e-commerce, with an in-depth analysis of the investor role in prospective consolidations.

Introduction

E-commerce in India has grown in leaps and bounds since its inception. India was touted as the fastest-growing e-commerce market globally this year;[1] according to an ASSOCHAM-Forrester study, it is growing at an annual rate of 51% and is expected to be valued at $120

---

[1] Phil Harpur, "India - Fixed Broadband, Digital Economy and Digital Media - Statistics and Analyses," BuddeComm focus report profile, last modified May 18, 2018, https://www.budde.com.au/Research/India-Fixed-Broadband-Digital-Economy-and-Digital-Media-Statistics-and-Analyses.

billion in 2020, up from just $30 billion in 2016.[2] It is therefore inevitably going to play an important role in India's economy and must be regulated so as to ensure that the boons outweigh the banes in the long run.

This article, admittedly future-focused, discusses the uncharted territories of regulation and the increasing need for such regulation in the e-commerce space—particularly regarding mergers and acquisitions (M&A) in e-commerce and the rising anti-trust issues that the Competition Commission of India (CCI) may have overlooked in various judgments. This article will also discuss various measures taken by other competition authorities to regulate these combinations and the trends that have been observed in other countries' e-commerce M&A.

There is no doubt that a country like India, housing the world's youngest population, would create the perfect breeding ground for e-commerce transactions. Conducting businesses online in India is seemingly easy with its favourable foreign trade and foreign investment policies. The rate at which internet penetration is growing shows just how comfortable Indians are with using the internet.[3] It goes without saying that more and more people are receptive to the idea of making purchases online, and such growth only means that the e-commerce market is here to stay.[4]

The ultimate purpose of this article is to enable creative thinking and to provide foresight on how under-deterrence of this market could lead to what the Commission is trying to prevent in the first place. The contention of the authors is that a market at its nascent stage must be freely competitive and therefore avoid any factors that could lead to concentration of the said market. Consolidations that have already begun in a market at such an early stage, with few competitors, raise suspicion that such behaviour could lead to concentration of the market, which would pave the way for a monopoly and could adversely affect the interests of consumers. A monopoly at such an early stage creates barriers to entry, which goes against the idea of free competition in the market. The market must serve

---

[2] "Indian Retail Industry- Structure & Prospects," Care Ratings, last modified June 2, 2017, http://www.careratings.com/upload/NewsFiles/SplAnalysis/Indian%20Retail%20Industry%20-%20June%202017.pdf.

[3] "E-Commerce," India Brand Equity Foundation, last modified July 2017, https://www.ibef.org/download/Ecommerce-July-2017.pdf. The compound annual growth rate (CAGR) of internet users in India is 15.6%, which would represent an increase from 391.50 million in 2016 to 700 million by 2020.

[4] According to the ASSOCHAM study, the number of purchases made online in India in the year 2016 was 69 million. This is expected to cross the 100 million mark by the end of 2017 and increase by 65% in the year 2018.

as an incubator for growth of new entrants, and it must not discourage them by seeming hostile.

The authors also contend, however, that monopoly by virtue of the natural outcome of a superior product or business acumen must not be of any concern to the competition authorities; that being said, the current players in the e-commerce space have not established a distinguishable, undifferentiated or superior product, nor have they maximised consumer welfare. Monopolies at this stage will therefore only adversely affect competition and result in lack of innovation, among other things.

Concerns[5] have also been raised about the lack of transparency regarding how consumers' data will be used after a successful merger or acquisition. Competition lawyers have mentioned that with the increased importance that e-commerce firms place in consumers' data, the lack of transparency pertaining to how the firms handle such data after an acquisition is a reason for the regulators to look into the potential threats that this could pose, and, in time, personal data "may well become a competition issue."[6]

The main goal of anti-trust laws must be consumer welfare. In the past few years, many mergers that took place between big players in the e-commerce space were, without any hesitation, given the nod by the CCI mainly because the Commission wanted to encourage the growth of this industry. In this process, it overlooked a few probable anti-competitive issues, emphasising that the market is in its nascent stage and over-deterrence would kill its wings before it could fly.

The decisions taken by the CCI, *prima facie*, seem to be beneficial in promoting the growth of the e-commerce industry; however, if this practice continues, it could lead to concentration of the industry and would undermine the purpose of competition law. The CCI must therefore adopt

---

[5] The EU Commission stated that Facebook's acquisition of WhatsApp could lead to data concentration, which will give Facebook's advertising market an edge over other similar markets. Similarly, the Delhi High Court in the WhatsApp Data Privacy case also expressed its concern over the sharing of personal information of WhatsApp users with Facebook after the latter acquired it. The petition was dismissed on the grounds that, since right to privacy was still an undecided matter, the petition was not amenable with the Court's writ jurisdiction. Now that right to privacy has been declared a fundamental right, the protection of usage of consumer data by the merged company/ies must be looked into by the regulators.

[6] Joaquin Almunia, "Competition and Personal Data Protection," European Commission SPEECH/12/860, November 26, 2012, http://europa.eu/rapid/press-release_SPEECH-12-860_en.htm.

such measures as are neither under-deterrent nor over-deterrent but are a perfect synthesis of the two.

M&A Trends in the E-commerce Industry

A total of 71 M&A took place in India during January–June 2017, according to a report by the H1 2017 Indian Startup Funding Report.[7] Fintech, healthcare and e-commerce took the top three slots with respect to the number of deals.[8]

Bangalore-based e-commerce giant Flipkart has grown since its inception in 2007 by acquiring several companies like Mime360 (2011), Letsbuy.com (2012), Myntra.com (2014) and Appiterate (2015), to name a few. Flipkart-owned-Myntra also acquired Jabong right after Amazon's US$1.2 billion deal with Jabong fell through for undisclosed reasons. Recently, Flipkart also acquired eBay for US$450 million as part of a cash-and-stock deal. It downed the shutters on Letsbuy.com in less than a year after acquiring it. Acquiring to wipe out a brand is not unusual in business, but the speed with which Letsbuy, as a brand, was exterminated shows that Flipkart is keen to strengthen its brand, no holds barred.

Amazon's golden ticket into the Indian market was through the acquisition of Indian based e-commerce platform Junglee.com. Its decision to shut down Junglee.com comes at a time when speculations have arisen that Amazon, Flipkart and Alibaba (through its stake in Paytm and Snapdeal) seem to be the only players in the market.

In today's day and age, M&A happen at the drop of a hat, but this was not always the case. There was a time when mergers were treated with a presumption of illegality. So what changed? It is crucial to understand and trace the evolution and reason behind this change, which will be explained in the next section of this article.

Harvard v. Chicago

Anti-trust analysis is now poised at a critical tipping point between the Harvard and the Chicago schools.[9] One can easily determine the outcome

---

[7] "Decoding The Merger And Acquisitions Trends in Indian Startup Ecosystem [H1 2017]," INC42, last modified July 25, 2017, https://inc42.com/buzz/startup-mergers-acquisitions-trends/.

[8] "Decoding The Merger And Acquisitions Trends," INC42.

[9] Thomas A. Piraino Jr., "Reconciling the Harvard and Chicago Schools- A New Antitrust Approach for the 21st Century," *Indiana Law Journal* 82, no. 2, Article 4 (Spring 2007).

of their case if they know which school the judge will swear by. The Harvard school is known to be more skeptical about innovation and seemingly "anti-competitive" practices that could ultimately benefit the consumers, whereas the Chicago school is known to take a more liberal approach and permit collusions that may have actually harmed the consumers. The Harvard school dominated the era of anti-trust analysis from the mid-20th century till the 1970s. Soon after, the Chicago school took over to counter the drawbacks of the Harvard school.

The Harvard School

Economists under this school were appalled by a concentrated market, even if it could potentially benefit the end-consumers. They argued that mergers in such a market could induce them to indulge in anti-competitive practices.[10] There was a presumption of illegality in the conduct of powerful firms when the market was concentrated. They did not trouble themselves with entering into complex economic analysis of the market, its players and the impact on the consumers. This was referred to as the "*per se* rule"; in other words, the conduct was deemed "*per se* illegal" as the anti-competitive potential seemed fairly obvious.[11] Economists Kaysen and Turner were consistently voicing their distrust of powerful firms, and they insisted on the restriction of market power and the need for it being the central focus on anti-trust policies. They were convinced that mergers would increase prices, decrease output, and reduce quality and innovation.

It is not unsurprising that this rigid approach was highly criticised by economists who believed in a free market with minimal government intervention, directed solely by "the law of demand and supply".

The Chicago School

This school believed that the only object of anti-trust legislations is "consumer welfare". There was a shift from the "presumption of illegality" method to one where the plaintiffs had to empirically prove that the firm was harming consumer welfare by increasing prices and decreasing output; this was deemed the "rule of reason".[12] In the case of *United States v. General*

---

[10] Turner, Donald F., "The Role of the 'Market Concept' in Antitrust Law," 49 *Antitrust Law Journal* 1145-1154 (March 1980).

[11] Herbert Hovenkamp, "Antitrust Policy, Restricted Distribution, and the Market for Exclusionary," *Minnesota Law Review* 71 (1986–87).

[12] When a company limited competition among distributors of TV sets, the judge held that the "potential economic benefit of the location clause imposed by

Dynamics Corporation,[13] the court held that a merger cannot be illegal only because it would have a high market share. It is imperative to consider the condition that might affect the future market share of merging parties.

In another landmark decision, the court permitted the merger of two out of the three major players in the airlines industry while stating that since the acquired company was under financial distress it no longer constituted a meaningful competitive force in the relevant market, even though it would lead to further market concentration[14] in the name of consumer welfare through the introduction of better products.

Their approach was similar to the Darwinian principle of "survival of the fittest". Monopolies are not to be *per se* declared illegal. Mergers with the intent to develop businesses and superior products and foster heightened business acumen must not be prohibited. Only wilful acquisitions to maintain or create monopoly power are anti-competitive.[15]

Despite all efforts, the Chicago school has failed to concretely demonstrate a merger's capacity to achieve economies of scale and cost reduction that will ultimately reduce prices. Courts also found it problematic to frame objective standards for determining the intent behind a merger.

Need for a Synthesis

The Post-Chicago school recognised the flaws of both the existing schools and decided to use a combined approach. For the first time, the court in *California Dental Association v. FTC*[16] indicated its willingness to combine the Harvard and the Chicago schools. It was believed that certain market structures were definitely capable of having anti-competitive consequences. The Chicago theory failed to recognise that, in reality, markets do not work perfectly. The existence of an even playing field is a far-fetched assumption. "Barriers to entry" is a reality.

This school recognised that monopolists are capable of leveraging their products into other markets or even preventing entries. It is necessary that courts deter monopolies from engaging in certain conduct which may

---

Sylvania Inc. is rule of reason." Continental T. V. Inc. v. GTE Sylvania Inc., 433 U.S. 36 (1977).

[13] United States v. General Dynamics Corporation, 415 U.S.486 (1974).

[14] In re: Boeing Co., [1997-2001 FTC Complaints & Orders Transfer Binder] Trade Reg. Rep. (CCH), 24, 123-24 (July 1, 1997).

[15] United States v. Grinnell Corp., 384 U.S. 563 (1966).

[16] California Dental Association v. FTC, 224 F.3d 942 (9th Cir. 2000).

generally be permitted for smaller firms. The new approach followed by the courts is that the conduct of the firm is studied under a continuum. The judges will no longer be forced to pick one side; they may presume illegality, or even conduct market analysis, as per the merits of the case. The quality of proof required should vary with the circumstances.[17]

Redefining the "Relevant Market" for the E-Commerce Industry

According to section 2(r) of the Competition Act, 2002, "relevant market" is defined as "the market which may be determined by the Commission with reference to 'relevant product market' or 'relevant geographic market' or with reference to both the markets."[18]

The power of defining the "relevant market" is left up to the sole discretion of the Commission and is decided on a case-by-case basis. This definition is the pretext to determine whether a firm is engaging in anti-competitive behaviour or is abusing its dominance in the relevant market. The more broadly a court defines "relevant market", the less likely it is for the defendant to exercise monopoly power in it.[19] Competitive constraints acting on the merging firms pre- and post-merger would therefore define the market. It must indicate the ability of the merged entity to engage in coordinated anti-competitive conduct post-merger. This section will discuss the current definition of "relevant market" adopted by the Commission while determining competition in the e-commerce industry.

Current Definition of "Relevant Market"

The authors argue that the current anti-trust laws were designed to regulate competition in more traditional markets. This is evidenced by the orders given in cases such as those of Mohit Manglani[20] and Snapdeal,[21]

---

[17] California Dental Association v. FTC, 526 U.S. 756 (1999).

[18] The Competition Act, 2002, No. 12 of 2003, sec. 2(r).

[19] Jared Kagan, "Bricks, Mortar and Google: Defining the Relevant Antitrust Market for Internet-based Companies," *New York Law School Law Review* 55 (2010): 273.

[20] Mohit Manglani v. M/S Flipkart India Private Limited & Ors., Case No. 80/2014, available at http://www.cci.gov.in/sites/default/files/802014.pdf, (hereinafter referred to as "Mohit Manglani case").

[21] Ashish Ahuja v. Snapdeal.com through Mr. Kunal Bahl, CEO & Ors., Case No. 17/2014 available at http://www.cci.gov.in/sites/default/files/172014.pdf, (hereinafter referred to as "Snapdeal case").

where the judges held that e-commerce and brick-and-mortar stores are mere distribution channels of the same retail market because they sell the same product.

In the Snapdeal case, Ashish Ahuja, the informant, filed a petition against Snapdeal and SanDisk for restricting his right to carry on his business of selling SanDisk's pen drives, hard drives, laptops and similar products on the e-commerce website. He urged the Commission to examine the actions of the opposite party and observe that they contravened sections 3[22] and 4[23] of the Act. The Commission held that offline and online markets only differ in certain aspects like discounts and shopping experiences and that, because they sell the same product, that they are two different channels of distribution but not two different markets. Consequently, because e-commerce only forms a negligible percentage of the overall retail market, it was hard to prove that Snapdeal, although one of the big players in the market, was abusing its dominance.

Similarly, in the Mohit Manglani case, the Commission ignored the barefaced anti-competitive conduct of e-commerce websites that entered into exclusive dealing agreements with sellers of goods/services. They based their rationale on the notion that since e-commerce forms a negligible share of the retail market these e-portals cannot be said to have abused any sort of dominance.

The above cases show that, so far, the Indian competition law does not recognise e-tail and retail as different markets; however, a welcome shift of this perception was observed in the Ola and Uber cases. It is generally advised to define the market such that the products are fairly substitutable. The taxi giants contended that the Commission must consider all modes of transport that constraint the competition on its taxis, like buses and autos; however, the Commission noted that the taxi model had facilities like point-to-point pickup, round-the-clock availability, GPRS tracking, ease of payment, professional drivers, good-quality vehicles, and predictability in journey and waiting time. It would be fallacious to submit that buses are alternatives for taxis at this point. In doing so, the Commission rightly delineated the market as one for radio taxis. Certainly, if the relevant market accommodated all modes of travel, the taxi giants' market shares would be insignificant.

---

[22] Anti-competitive agreements.— No enterprise or association of enterprises or person or association of persons shall enter into any agreement in respect of production, supply, distribution, storage, acquisition or control of goods or provision of services, which causes or is likely to cause an appreciable adverse effect on competition within India.

[23] Abuse of dominant position.

The implication of the ratio of the Snapdeal and Mohit Manglani judgments is worrisome to say the least. It is undeniable that e-commerce and brick-and-mortar stores have a thin line difference, but this subtle difference cannot be ignored, for reasons which will be stated in the next section.

Need to Redefine the Market

Going by the above definition of "relevant market", e-commerce only has a slender share of the total retail market. In 2014, it accounted for 0.5%[24] of the retail market; it shot up to 2.5%[25] in the year 2016, which is a record increase of 400%. Clearly, the e-commerce industry is not to be taken lightly. E-commerce is currently, on the face of it, making its investors and consumers happy, but might we remind you of the boom and bust fiasco of the internet from the late 1990s to the early 2000s? People pinned all their hopes on the dot-com business (Why wouldn't they? Just adding ".com" apparently quadrupled profits of various companies.); everybody thought that it was a good replacement for the traditional way of handling businesses, but it backfired. If history serves as a precursor to help avoid past mistakes, then unprecedented growth of anything, be it internet or real estate (after the 2000s), can cause adverse effects.

The concept of "relevant market" is a cornerstone of competition law and thus should be defined scientifically and dynamically. Unfortunately, the Commission has time and again defined "relevant market" in a rigid manner without considering that e-commerce and offline stores are fundamentally different in that e-commerce is a product of innovation and offline stores are a concoction of man, money and material (land). The US Federal Trade Commission and the EU Competition Authority now treat e-tail and retail as separate markets, so as to not let unfair practices go unnoticed by firms that hide behind a farrago of distortions. Store owners can establish trust among their customers by way of setting up a lavish store (the investment demonstrates the seller's commitment to stay in the

---

[24] Divye Sharma, "Competition Law And E-Commerce: A Concern For The Future," *Mondaq*, last updated May 27, 2015, http://www.mondaq.com/india/x/400368/Antitrust+Competition/Competition+Law+And+ECommerce+A+Concern+For+The+Future.

[25] "Fulfilled! India's e-commerce retail logistics growth story," KPMG, last updated August 2016, https://assets.kpmg.com/content/dam/kpmg/in/pdf/2016/08/E-commerce-retail-logistics-India.pdf.[26] Flipkart is being compared with a shopping mall because they both offer a wide array of products/services.

market); however, it is harder to establish trust in the e-commerce market. There is a wide array of things that need to be achieved by this sector; for instance, protection of consumer data and transparency in price. The customers that e-commerce caters to are different from those of traditional outlets, the former catering to people who have access to technology.

Theoretically, if e-commerce were a freely competitive market where e-portals would have to fight for the market, market power would mean nothing. This is because adoption of e-commerce has paved the way for a fast-moving market which is characterised by high innovation and technology, meaning that anybody with superior technology could surpass an incumbent's "established" market power. Courts would then find it difficult to establish dominance in such a fickle industry, which serves to prove that the concerned authorities must make new regulations which are not primarily based on a firm's market power. Through wide-scale acquisitions, however, incumbent firms are trying to render the market less competitive, creating barriers to entry, *inter alia*. The need to redefine the "relevant market" is more important now than ever.

Lastly, most online portals have services that are entirely different than the services provided by brick-and-mortar stores. If one were to compare Flipkart and a shopping mall,[26] the former can provide services to enhance a person's shopping experience that shopping malls cannot and vice-versa.[27] The Commission has intermittently stated that it under-deters the e-commerce market to promote economic growth. A market can grow only when there is free competition. The wide-scale consolidations have led to a concentrated market, which hinders competition. This is because the Commission has undermined the potential of this market, thereby allowing widespread M&A which could lead to an increase in price and a decrease in quality, output and innovation. The regulators must strive to look at these cases in a continuum instead of applying outdated principles and define the "relevant market" in a dynamic way.

The only way to deter anti-trust issues that could arise from premature mergers and acquisitions is to realise that the e-commerce market is different from offline markets. The authors opine that in order to allow free competition in this market, consolidations among players must be

---

[26] Flipkart is being compared with a shopping mall because they both offer a wide array of products/services.

[27] Flipkart provides home-delivery services, with the convenience of shopping at home on the computer or through an application on a smartphone. Similarly, malls give customers the whole shopping experience, allowing them to try on products before actually buying them, among other things.

strictly regulated to see whether they could lead to barriers of entry or concentration of the market, which can only be successful when e-commerce is treated as a separate market. Another implication would be that even if the e-commerce player is indulging in anti-competitive practices it will always escape liability simply because the court has too broadly defined the "relevant market".

Adverse Effects of Premature Consolidations in the E-Commerce Market

Monopoly

Although some bigwigs of the e-commerce industry may be in a position to abuse their dominance, they hide behind the façade of an inflated market definition to show that they are unimportant players; market concentration goes unnoticed because of this façade.

The one truth of economics that the Commission has ignored is that monopolists lie to escape the risks of being closely scrutinised. They frame their market as a union of several large markets in order to conceal their monopoly.[28] This is essentially what Google does. It disguises its market power by saying it is a union of several other markets.[29]

Artificial monopolies are usually established on the foundation of a superior product, a novel innovation or a product that is easily differentiated from others in the market, and such monopolies are established over a long period of time. E-commerce portals, however, have not had enough time to evolve into a mature market. The authors believe that technological superiority should be the qualification of a monopolist. That being said, the authors concede that monopolies deserve their bad reputation only in a world where nothing changes.[30] Creative monopolies give customers more choice by adding entirely new categories of products,

---

[28] Google is known for calling itself just another tech-company; fortunately, the Commission recognised its tactic and, in an investigation it conducted in 2014 into Google's activities, it recognised that Google was indulging in anti-competitive behaviour by giving way to a search bias. Google's contention was that its relevant market was "information", which would include social networking sites, online and offline encyclopaedias. Far from dominant, that would make it irrelevant in that market. The Director General, however, realised that Google had more than an 85% share in web-searches from 2009–2014 and therefore was dominant and abused this dominance in terms of Section 4 of the Competition Act, 2002 (India).

[29] Peter Thiel, Blake Masters, *Zero to One* , Virgin Books, London (2014).

[30] Thiel, *Zero to One*, (see n. 29).

and they are great only if they can endure in the future.[31] The problem arises only when the monopoly is earned without any apparent merit, as consolidations in this case are not to provide superior products for customers but merely done because the monopolists have the means to acquire another company. Moore's law[32] is usually used to describe the absence of monopoly in high-technology markets, rendering the need for anti-trust laws in such markets unnecessary and obsolete.

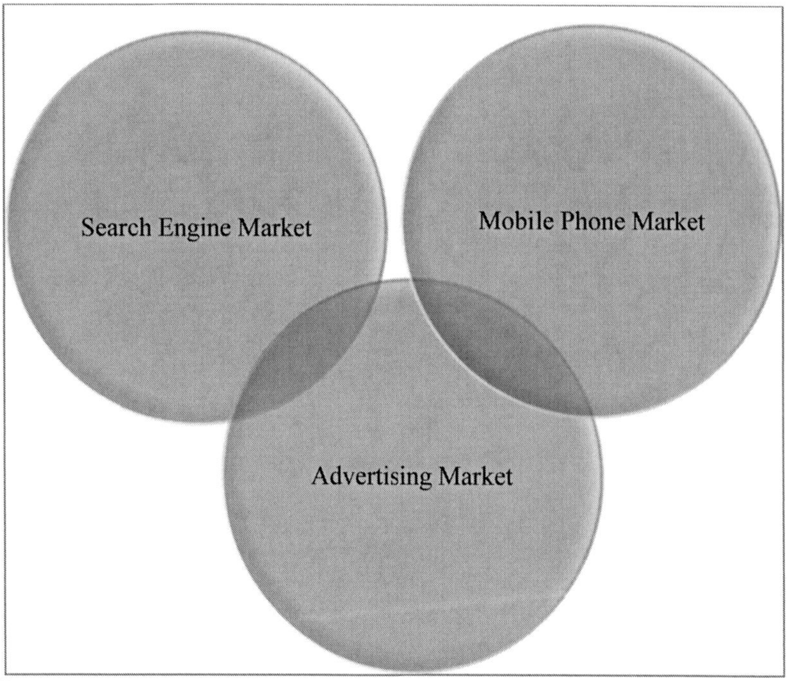

33

---

[31] According to Joseph Schumpeter, few participants will persist until the "gales of creative destruction" lead to market displacement. SeeIlene Knable, Scott Sher, and Michele Lee, "Antitrust Merger Analysis in High-Technology Markets," *European Competition Journal* 4, no. 2 (2008): 464.

[32] Moore's Law is named after Gordon E. Moore, the co-founder of Fairchild Semiconductor, who described the phenomenon in a 1965 article in Electronics Magazine: "The power of a silicon chip will double every eighteen to twenty-four months, accelerating the rate of technological advances."

[33] Search engine ∪ Mobile phones ∪ Advertising.

In the e-commerce market, sustaining a monopoly is nearly impossible because of the dynamic nature of technology and the ease with which someone can enter the market with a far superior product than that of the incumbent. Having said that, these firms, by way of consolidations and anti-competitive agreements, extend their monopolies by leveraging into different markets and by taking undue advantage of network effects.[34] The problem with high-technology monopolies and mergers stems not from their achievement of market power but from their misuse of it; therefore, courts should only penalise artificial monopoly.

Leveraging into Different Markets

It is well-established that a monopoly could make greater profit if it also owned complementary markets.[35] As long as a firm feels that its market power can be challenged, it will continue to seek efficiency gains. As discussed above, a firm in the e-commerce market never has a stagnant market share, and so firms opt to acquire other businesses that are complementary to their own primary businesses. This phenomenon is evidenced by the trends of players like Flipkart establishing a foothold in the electronics industry and the fashion industry through its acquisitions, Amazon India pledging US$500 million for expansion of its food retail business, and the fact that Uber and Ola are entering into the realm of food delivery.

Network Effects

Economies of scale in consumption may also play a significant role in extending the duration of a high-technology monopoly; this is known as "network effects". In order to be successful, a new network must convince a large number of the installed base of users to migrate from the incumbent network. Network effects are present in most high-technology markets and are often the reason behind monopolies in these markets.[36] When such a market has multiple service providers, it is clear that

[34] This could also be a way for them to unfairly prolong their monopoly status, which would be unethical.

[35] See Michael A. Salinger, *Introduction to Chapters VII and IX of Augustin Cournot: Review of Mathematical Principles of the Theory of Wealth by Augustin Cournot* (The Macmillan Company, 1838).

[36] Alan Murray, "Intellectual Property: Old Rules Don't Apply," WALL ST. J. (August 2001).

everyone benefits from using the same product.[37]First-mover advantage is high in markets capable of high network effects. Regulators should not bank on innovations to create a market displacement.

Two-sided Markets

In simple terms, it is business that facilitates the interaction of two parties that were previously less accessible to one another for various reasons, such as high transaction costs. This is found in e-commerce markets. Usually, products and services are offered for "free" and the other side subsidises them.[38] Network effects enable a large network to become dominant, thus making it difficult for new entrants to challenge the incumbents. The larger the network, the easier it is for both side participants to match their wants.[39] This is why there is aggressive competition in the market—so that the consumers settle for one or few enterprises.

Countervailing Powers of the Buyer

It is the presence of power which mitigates the consequence of consumer surplus that would arise from a horizontal merger. Its existence proves the presence of competitive constraints. If the buyer can reduce or threaten to reduce his/her purchase from the merged entity through switching to rivals, buyer power exists. Consolidations will quite obviously reduce this power as it would eliminate rivals that one can choose from. A merger is known to be anti-competitive when it reduces this power.

Cab Aggregators

Start-ups have leveraged the mobile internet to create a platform that links drivers and riders through incentives and discounts, thereby correcting the weakness of traditional taxi markets. With the growing

---

[37] For instance, if there are hundreds of social networking sites, and each has just few users, the consumers will not benefit from this as having one platform where everyone visits will more efficiently facilitate their need to network. This is due to the network effects present in the market.

[38] For instance, in online retail, buyers are allowed to freely use the websites, whereas sellers have to pay a certain price to list their products on the platform.

[39] For instance, buyers will benefit from more sellers, and sellers will benefit from more buyers.

consumer acceptance of this luxurious mode of travel, India has become a battleground for global cab aggregators.

The Chinese Debacle

China is a start-up favourite, as it houses the largest market for smartphone users and a fast-growing ride-hailing market. Naturally, it enticed global giants like San Francisco-based Uber Inc. to enter the market. Uber found itself in a fierce battle with the local favourite, Didi Dache. When Uber made its appearance in 2013, it had a market share of about 8%.[40] Owing to its venture capital support, it engaged in a capital dumping strategy to lure drivers and customers through attractive incentives and discounts; but alas, like all American dreams that died in China,[41] or perhaps on account of Didi's home-court advantage, Uber faced losses of around $200 million every month and decided to give up its operations to Didi. According to various sources, the merged entity would be valued at around $35 billion. Uber will have a 17.7% stake in Didi, which includes a 5.89% share of the combined entity. Didi will in turn invest a whopping $1 billion in Uber's global operations.[42]This deal was an investor favourite, as the battle turned uglier by the minute, with extensive capital spending, which made both the companies unprofitable. Many believed that this would encourage Didi, now the sole market player,[43] to focus on providing the users with a better experience. This did not happen.

Reports show that 24 hours after the merger took place, the cost of hailing a cab increased exponentially. A report by *Beijing Business Today* said that immediately after the merger Didi ended the subsidies provided

---

[40] Tracey Lien, Paresh Dave and Julie Makinen, "Uber China to join rival Didi Chuxing in $35-billion deal," *Los Angeles Times*, August 1, 2016, http://www.latimes.com/business/technology/la-fi-tn-uber-didi-20160731-snap-story.html.

[41] Amazon, not able to compete, eventually started selling its products through Alibaba and tech-giants like Google and Facebook are not allowed to operate in China. Even eBay lost out to Alibaba.

[42] Alyssa Abkowitz, "Uber Sells China Operations to Didi Chuxing," *Wall Street Journal*, August 1, 2016, https://www.wsj.com/articles/china-s-didi-chuxing-to-acquire-rival-uber-s-chinese-operations-1470024403.

[43] Uber will still remain an independent brand, running in its own name in China. However, recent reports show that Didi's imprints are evident in Uber's apps, shortly after the resignation of Uber CEO.

to drivers.[44] Many customers took to social media to complain about the doubling of fares, which has incentivised them to pick cheaper modes of travel like carpooling and public transportation. Now that there is no need to fight for the top spot, Didi has no incentive to pour money into promotional activities. Consumers are left with no choice but to either accept the prices or pick public transportation. This is ever more troubling for loyal customers who have become accustomed to the luxury of cabs.[45] A study concluded that the "response rate" during peak hours reduced considerably, perhaps due to the lack of incentives provided to the drivers.

At times like these, companies look out for new beginner drivers who are willing to work without extravagant incentives; however, in a surprising turn of events, it seems like the regulatory measures adopted, like local *hukou*,[46] and vehicle and license plate registrations, acted as an entry barrier of sorts. Car plates in Shanghai and Beijing are notorious for being difficult to acquire. Many citizens have reported waiting years before they received theirs. Mofcom,[47] one of China's anti-trust regulators, has commented on the issue, saying that the merger would not be approved without a filing by the company. Concerns were raised that the merged entity would enjoy 90% of the market share, which is a clear red flag. In response, Didi stated that it has not triggered the $400 million limit required for the said filing, coupled with the fact that both the companies are loss-making entities in the Chinese market. The story is not all that different from the Indian scenario right now. Didi, in order to be resilient against Uber's advances, absorbed Kuaidi Dache, a local competitor. Similarly, Ola acquired TaxiForSure, only to shut it down. On record, it was a cost-cutting measure that relieved it from around Rs. 30 crores per month; but the question that no one is asking is whether it was an attempt to buy out and demolish a competitor. It is a common practice for big

---

[44] He Huifeng, "Ride hailing giant Didi Chuxing raises prices in China's biggest cities," *China Business*, last updated September 5, 2016, http://www.scmp.com/business/china-business/article/2015137/ride-hailing-giant-didi-chuxing-raises-prices-chinas-biggest.

[45] Based on a study conducted by Chinese web portal Sina, 81.7% of respondents believe that hailing a ride in China is more difficult than it was a year ago, and 86.7% say that it is more difficult than it ever has been. See Josh Horwitz, "One year after the Uber-Didi merger, it's only getting harder to hail a ride in China," *Quartz*, August 3, 2017,https://qz.com/1045268/one-year-after-the-uber-didi-merger-its-only-getting-harder-to-hail-a-ride-in-china/.

[46] A compulsory resident permit which implies that only residents of a particular city can operate in that city. This will make it difficult for non-citizen residents to obtain a license and ride the taxis.

[47] Ministry of Commerce, China.

firms to absorb the small ones to gain market power; but, if Ola was already facing losses due to high costs, why would it buy a company only to close it in a year?

Most companies seem to be using the stipulated “threshold” limit to escape the anti-trust watchdogs. Loss-making entities *prima facie* pose no threat of abusing their dominant position, as this is commonly attributed to a company rich in profits and market power; however, the scenario is different from the traditional markets that the law was originally based on. High-technology markets are known to reap profits only after 10to 15 years and actually remain unprofitable in the initial years. Uber and Didi have escaped the eyes of law merely on account of their losses; however, the consequence of their merger is enough to show that they must not be taken lightly. Moreover, China lacks a proper formula through which the combined turnover can be evaluated[48] for new business models like these. The takeaway from this is the fact that Uber now has this pent-up venture capital money to burn in India and show some tough competition to Ola. It is important to note that while regulations are necessary they must not hinder the innovation process that drives customers and drivers away from cab-hailing innovations back to the traditional modes of transportation. In high-technology markets, there is fierce competition in the nascent stages. It is advisable to have minimal government intervention as competition here is healthy, if not advisable. As the market matures, the regulators should step in. It is a stage where monopoly is inevitable because consumers demand one network standard. [49]The market power shifts to that player that owns the standard, leaving the others to slowly die out; therefore, it is paramount that this position is achieved freely and fairly, so when the inevitable happens it is the most deserved player that survives. This healthy competition will not even begin, however, if the smaller firms believe that a few have an unfair advantage.

That said, regulation is required if, in the nascent stages, there is no free competition. If the existing players are destroying small players and creating a hostile environment for new entrants, anti-trust supervision and regulation is welcome.[50]

---

[48] Wang Cong, “Didi-Uber merger doubts,” *Global Times*, http://www.globaltimes.cn/content/1004647.shtml.

[49] David A. Balto and Robert Pitofsky, “Antitrust and High-Tech Industries: The New Challenge,” *Antitrust Bulletin* 43 (1998): 604.

[50] This is why several state governments have amended their motor vehicle laws to legalise cab-aggregators and made various compliance mandates; however, they have failed to address key issues relating to anti-competition. One such provision which poses an obvious red-flag is the “residence requirement and knowledge of

It's always SON-NY in E-commerce

It all started when Didi Dache (lead investor Tencent) and Kuaidi Dache (lead investor Alibaba) announced their merger in 2015. Perhaps to combat the arrival of Uber, investors pushed for a merger; notably, SoftBank CEO Masonyoshi Son was an initial investor in Alibaba and held a large stake in Kuaidi. Subsequent to the merger, SoftBank held a large stake in the now-combined entity. Uber and Didi indulged in a fierce battle until the two called a truce, and the American company was acquired in 2016, making the combined entity, Didi Chuxing, the largest player in the market. Didi thus became a minority shareholder in Uber Inc., and Uber had a stake of approximately 20% in Didi. On the Indian front, Didi has been making investments in Ola. This put everyone in a fix because a significant investor now had a stake in Ola's arch-rival, Uber.

SoftBank is notorious for investing in competitors and creating some value out of everything; thus, it too has a stake (of 30%) in Ola. According to an Alibaba investor, Son has facilitated numerous mergers and always figured out how to win through consolidation. This is not an unprecedented event.

Recently, SoftBank pushed for a merger between two e-commerce players, Snapdeal and Flipkart, which ultimately failed; however, unflustered by Snapdeal's decision to recreate its avatar as a standalone company, Son has agreed to invest[51] in the leading player, Flipkart. SoftBank also pushed for a merger between Snapdeal's subsidiary (FreeCharge) and Paytm, which also eventually failed.[52] Another mutual investor is the venture capital wing of Tiger Global, which has invested in all three—Didi Chuxing, Ola and Uber.

In another turn of events, SoftBank has agreed to invest $10 billion in Uber Inc. (as of November 2017), which will also attract several corporate governance changes and earn them a seat on the board of Uber Inc. and a promise of an IPO by 2019. This means that SoftBank has a significant stake in the largest ride-hailing companies in India. Interestingly, it has invested in ride-hailing giants all around the world—without knowing who will be the winner, it will definitely have a stake in one of them.

Owing to the increasing number of mutual investors among the two, is there a possibility for a merger between Ola and Uber? Eventually, the fight over dominance is going to get costlier. Investors will expect to see

---

kannada mandate" in the Karnataka Regulation, which was recently upheld by the High Court.

[51] They have pumped $2.5 billion into Flipkart after the failed deal.

[52] However, they decided to pump $1.4 million into Paytm after the failed deal.

profits at some point, let alone cherish a dream of an IPO. It will all boil down to how these companies use their money—perhaps innovation for the benefit of consumers. Should this merger happen, the combined entity will have an easy 90% share in the market.

Anti-trust watchdogs are well advised to err on the side of caution.[53] It is also possible that the potential merger will be well timed, at a stage when there are no potential new entrants as they have all either retreated due to losses or been absorbed by one of the giants. This means that the merging parties would be at liberty to take back all incentives and promotions as capital dumping will eventually lead to cost-recovery strategies. That said, this is not the only possibility. Investors may encourage them to stop undercutting one another and take steps to make some profits. In fact, this is evidenced by the reduction in discounts and driver-incentives in the wake of 2017.

Soon enough, the duopolists will realise that the winner does not really take it all and the price war will lead them nowhere. According to popular economics, the criteria for this fabled phenomenon are:

Strong cross-side network effect: The availability of drivers willing to accept the ride will increase the number of riders. Similarly, when more riders book rides drivers will be able to meet their daily ride requirements and earn incentives. This is a strong cross-side network effect.

Positive same-side network effect: As the market grows and there is disparity in demand and supply, the problem of negative same-side effect is seen. As more drivers join, they compete to serve a rider, and vice-versa; however, the companies have tried to solve this problem by introducing carpooling options,[54] which, as an added bonus, means low prices for riders and more earnings for the drivers.

High switching cost: Both riders and drivers are not locked into any one operator, so they are at liberty to use either of the apps as they please. This means the switching cost is non-existent.

On perusal, two of the three conditions required for a winner-take-all model are not present. When the rivals—or worse, the investors—realise this, their price war will seem futile, and this could potentially lead to dangerous cost-recovery strategies or even consolidation.

---

[53] While legally there are no restrictions on venture capitalists investing in competing firms, it is a moral grey area.

[54] Like Ola Share and Uber Pool.

Meru Cabs and Fast Track Cabs vs. ANI Technologies

This case was filed by Meru and Fast Track Call Cabs against OlaCabs, a radio taxi service that had allegedly abused its dominant position in the market by offering deep discounts and incentives to customers and drivers.[55] The Director General (DG) demarcated the relevant market satisfactorily—distinguishing them from the usual public transport. It analysed the market power of Ola in the relevant market during the period from June 2012 until September 2015 to determine whether it held a dominant position.[56] There was an obvious decrease in the incumbent firms' market share on the arrival of Ola;[57] however, its fast growth was hindered by the entrance of the global giant Uber Inc. in 2013.[58]

The DG opined that, in order to have a "dominant position", it is necessary to hold a high market share for a reasonable amount of time. However, Ola's share has been significantly reducing after the entry of Uber.[59] The CCI's view that the network created by the opposite party, though admittedly large, was not large enough to prevent Uber from making its advances and gain a substantial position in the market is painfully parochial. The only reason Uber was able to achieve the same is

---

[55] The Director General was asked to investigate this matter by the Competition Commission as there seemed to be *prima facie* evidence of the alleged abuse. The DG correctly observed that despite Ola being an "aggregator of cabs" and not an asset-based business model the two were functionally substitutable and this would come under the realm of radio taxis.

[56] The DG observed that the market power of the existing players like Meru, Mega Cabs, Easy Cabs and the Karnataka State Transport Development Corporation declined substantially during this period. In 2012, when it entered, Ola's market share was 5–6%; in 2015–2016 it increased to 61–62%.

[57] Meru was in the lead till mid-2014, after which Ola was the clear dominator.

[58] Uber had entered the market in 2013 and had a market share of about 1–2% in the year 2013–2014. In 2014–2015, it was 20–22%; however, in March 2015 Uber was in 2nd position behind Ola. Uber's trip size grew 1,200% from January to September 2015, whereas Ola's growth during the same period was 63%. In the first half of 2015, Ola's market share increased marginally by 2–3%, whereas Uber's marginal growth was 22%.

[59] In 2015, Ola raised Rs. 2,059 crores by September and Rs. 3,445 crores by December 2015. Uber's capital is far greater and is said to be 15–20 times more than Ola's. These figures have only increased tremendously in 2017.Due to their respective capital supports, the gap in market share narrowed from 69% in January 2015 to 22% in September 2015.

because of its high-capital backing,[60] which by no means is comparable to the capabilities of the incumbents.

While it may be true that the capital requirement to start up a company is low in this market, it takes a lot to attract customers who are already loyal to incumbents because of the network effects. The reason Uber was able to do this was because of its capital backing. Is this not a barrier to entry?

The Commission rightly pointed out that the switching cost involved is minimal, so neither of them can completely lock customers or drivers; however, that is only when there is competition. When one of them surrenders, which is definitely possible, there may be no suitable alternative to switch to.

Coming to the problem of barriers due to access to alternative investment funds, the Commission gave a very unsatisfactory answer; it stated that the traditional concept of "capital requirements" is not fully applicable here and that the instrumental elements in success are the fiercely competitive environment, fast adaptation to changes and constant innovation in business models.[61] If that is so, why are new start-ups (with a more creative model) like Hyhop and Utoo still floundering at best?

Strangest of all, the Commission opined that most new entrants engage in practices like exclusive dealings, below-cost pricing and loyalty discounts to gain a toehold in the market. It sounds like the DG has simply cloaked the predatory pricing tactic with business jargon. This practice has clearly edged out incumbents and slowed down new entrants. The Commission stated that the goal of competition law is to ensure that there is a wide variety of products available at reasonable prices, and regulatory intervention at this juncture is unwarranted to protect existing players or help new entrants; however, this too is short-sighted, as this price war will lead to cost-recovery strategies a few years down the line. One may argue that if the companies increase their prices, it could attract other entrants; however, they are going to have to match the low rates that the incumbents used to charge, and to do that one needs more capital. The vicious circle continues. The only way to break this is if they come up with yet another innovation and a cost-efficient model to naturally undercut the problem. Can we afford to wait for this?

The CCI should recognise the concept of collective dominance. In this regard, the Commission laid out some troubling technical glitches in the

---

[60] Its private equity links has enabled it to spend millions on discounts and incentives.

[61] Fast Track Call Cab Pvt. Ltd. v. ANI Technologies Pvt. Ltd., 2017 CompLR 667 (CCI).

law and disregarded this contention altogether. This article explicitly requests that the judiciary have a more expansive outlook with the changing times. If this problem is not nipped in the bud, we will witness an unwelcome unity of the two taxi giants.

Conclusion

Based on our understanding of the cases analysed, e-commerce giants have been absolved of their liabilities due to rigid technicalities such as the threshold limits[62] prescribed in the Act itself. The authors propose that the concept of a trigger-limit must be revisited. The nature of high-technology markets is such that a company sees profits only after a remarkable amount of time; further, loss-making firms can successfully combine in the e-commerce industry to overthrow incumbents.

Owing to the nascent stage of this market, regulation must be to a great enough extent to deter anti-competitive behaviour by making a thorough and in-depth analysis of the effects of a merger between the e-commerce players, and by observing the investor patterns to detect any personal consolidation agenda.[63] The terms of use of consumer data by a merged entity must also be recognised as an anti-trust issue. Ultimately, whether or not and how quickly regulation ought to be implemented should be decided on a case-by-case basis.

The crux of the matter is the definition of "relevant market". It is fundamentally fallacious to still believe that e-commerce is a subset of traditional markets. In conclusion, the authors would like to state that this "mergermania" must not go unnoticed and pave the way for a greater evil that is bound to occur.

---

[62] The Competition Act, 2002, No. 12 of 2003, sec. 5.

[63] See "It is always SON-ny in e-commerce"—A detailed explanation of how Softbank, which has invested in both Ola and Uber and has controlling stakes in the two, could possibly result in an unwanted merger of the two major players in the market.

CHAPTER V

MANDATORY OFFER REQUIREMENT IN TAKEOVER REGULATIONS: A CURSE IN DISGUISE?

TUSHAR KUMAR

Abstract

The Mandatory Offer Requirement (MOR) is a protective device inserted into the takeover laws of various jurisdictions to safeguard the interests of minority shareholders of the concerned target company. It imposes an obligation upon the investor to extend the initial investment offer to the rest of the shareholders so as to provide them a fair chance of exit and ensure equitable treatment of all shareholders; however, the possibly adverse implications of inclusion of such a measure are manifold. Firstly, MOR is based on the premise of a flawed assumption that the new controlling shareholder will be oppressive in its policies towards the rest of the shareholders. Secondly, the mechanism is unable to provide "effective protection" to the minority shareholders as its "trigger limit"; in other words, "control threshold" (positive or negative control) is a subjective criterion and is bound to be misused. Further, the obligation of extending the same offer to minority shareholders burdens the investor with huge capital obligations for an investment, thereby deterring many efficient takeovers in the economy and leading to the notion of MOR being "pro-minority" and "anti-takeover". Emphasising the integral role played by corporate takeovers in the economy, this essay throws light on the rigid nature of MOR which, in turn, enlarges the risk of an acquirer. The takeover laws of various jurisdictions, including India, have been analysed in this regard. The essay concludes by suggesting alternatives and possible reforms to the current mechanism of MOR in takeover codes of various countries, including invocation of MOR as a remedial measure by minority shareholders or the takeover regulatory body parting with the mandatory compliance of MOR and leaving it to the discretion of the respective target company.

Introduction

The MOR, also known as Mandatory Bid Rule in Europe[1] and elsewhere, is one of the central themes of the takeover regulations of most of the jurisdictions. It is a protective device, ideally meant for safeguarding the interests of minority shareholders of a target company (the company whose shares are being acquired), in case of its acquisition of shares or takeover. The requirement, triggered as soon as the investor crosses the "control threshold" (acquisition of control), imposes an obligation on the investor to extend the initial investment offer to the rest of the shareholders of the target company. The mechanism of MOR varies across jurisdictions, with most countries in Europe mandating the offer obligations for the rest of the shareholders, while some—like India—making open-offer obligations (equivalent to MOR) mandatory until 51% shareholding is achieved and optional after that.[2] The origin of MOR can be traced back to the City Code[3] enacted in the UK in 1968. In the late 20th century, owing to several instances of suppression of a minority by a majority,[4] the issue of preservation of interests of minority shareholders led to the amendment of the Code in 1974; this soon became the epochal theme of takeover regulations of both common-law and civil-law countries.[5] The major objectives of MOR are two-fold: to provide the right to exit for minority shareholders[6] and to ensure equitable treatment of all shareholders.[7] The ideal and practical facets of MOR fail to overlap by huge margins, as the obligations imposed on the investor, under the guise

---

[1] Directive 2004/25/EC on Takeover Bids, 2004 O.J. (L 142) 12 (EC), art. 5.

[2] Securities and Exchange Board of India (Substantial Acquisition of Shares and Takeovers) Regulations, 2011, reg. 7(1) (India).

[3] The City Code on Takeovers and Mergers, 1968 (UK).

[4] Foss v. Harbottle, 67 E.R. 189 (1843); Hogg v. Cramphorn, 3 All E.R. 4(1966); B. Howard Smith Ltd. v. Ampol Petroleum Ltd., 1 All E.R. 1126 (1974).

[5] Umakanth Varottil, "Comparative Takeover Regulation and the Concept of Control," *Singapore Journal of Legal Studies* (July 2015): 212.

[6] Alistair Defriez, Maurice Button, and Sarah Bolton, *A Practitioner's Guide to the City Code on Takeovers and Mergers* (City & Financial Publishing, 1999), 96–97.

[7] "OECD Principles of Corporate Governance," Organisation For Economic Co-Operation And Development, 1999, accessed November 15, 2017, http://www.oecd.org/officialdocuments/publicdisplaydocumentpdf/?cote=C/MIN(99)6&docLanguage=En.

of minority shareholders' protection, discourage many value-increasing and efficient transactions in the economy, not to overlook the significance of the rejuvenating role played by corporate takeovers. Further, offer requirements are a failure in providing "effective protection" to the interests of minority shareholders[8] as the trigger limit or the control threshold is an elusive concept and yet to be ascertained. Investing companies might therefore circumvent their transactions to avoid the regulatory requirements of the law.

Economic Relevance of Corporate Takeovers

Generally, the guiding vision of a corporation is to maximise profits, enhance shareholder wealth and achieve economic efficiency, thereby helping the economy to attain the point of optimum utilisation of resources.[9] From a practical point of view, however, the corporate entity cannot endure remaining in the stage of cost-effectiveness throughout its life, without bringing about a substantial change in its mechanism. Substantial acquisitions of shares and takeovers play a vital role by promoting efficiency through reallocating the economic resources of the enterprise.[10]

Darwin's theory of "survival of the fittest" has a bearing on the economic functioning of the enterprise as the market competitiveness leaves no room for complacency for an enterprise. Performance of a corporate entity is to be judged relatively, and the yardstick is the performance of other enterprises in the market. If a corporation is unable to cope with the competition, it will be taken over by various other competing industries looking out for any opportunity to increase their stake and expand their operations in the market. The threat of takeover as a pre-takeover measure is of paramount importance; when the incumbent management of the corporation has become incapable of extracting extra potential profits,[11] the threat acts as an incentive and induces it to either devise new policies favourable to performance or bring about the desired

---

[8] S. Kumarsundaram, "Corporate Takeovers: The Indian Situation," *Economic and Political Weekly* 18, no. 23 (June 1983): 1025.

[9] Lyman Johnson, "Corporate Takeovers And Corporations: Who Are They For?" *Washington and Lee Law Review* 43, (January 1986): 781.

[10] Donald C. Langevoort, "The Supreme Court and the Politics of Corporate Takeovers: A Comment on CTS Corp. v. Dynamics Corp. of America," *Harvard Law Review* 101, (December 1987): 96.

[11] Jesper Lau Hansen, "The Mandatory Bid Rule: The Rise to Prominence of a Misconception," *Scandinavian Studies in Law* 45, (2003): 176.

change in them (reducing agency costs thereby leading to higher price of shares),[12] lest it be the subject of acquisition by an investor. This notion has also been recognised by the Eggleston Committee report in 1969[13] as the core principle for the reform of the Australian takeover regulation.

On the other hand, reliable studies and empirical evidence document increased firm value as well as attainment of cost-effectiveness of the acquiring as well as the target companies in the post takeover scenario, thereby showing that takeovers contribute to the economy as a whole. The reasons for these gains emanating from the takeover activity can be numerous, ranging from combined goodwill of acquiring and target companies, and sound financial management strategies to heightened optimism among the investors following the takeover. A summary of the empirical work undertaken by economists Jensen and Ruback concluded that corporate takeovers generate positive gains for both the parties concerned in the investment,[14] and specifically 20–30% for the target firms on the announcement of a takeover bid.[15] Recently, Cavendish Industries witnessed quite a positive profit before tax and reduction of conversion costs a year after its acquisition by JK Tyre Industries, a Singhania unit.[16] Shares of Monnet Ispat & Energy rose by 17.05% amidst the speculations of its takeover by Steel Authority of India Limited (SAIL).[17] Change of management puts the existing resources or capital to better and more efficient use to match market competitiveness. The

---

[12] Easterbrook and Fischel, "The Proper Role of a Target's Management in Responding to a Tender Offer," *Harvard Law Review* 94, (1982): 1190–92.

[13] Second Interim Report of the Company Law Advisory Committee, Takeovers Panel, Government of Australia (February 1969), http://www.takeovers.gov.au/content/Resources/eggleston_committee/2nd_interim_report.aspx.

[14] M. C. Jensen and R.S. Ruback, "The Market For Corporate Control," *Journal of Financial Economics* 11, (April 1983): 5–50.

[15] Mary S. Schranz, "Takeovers Improve Firm Performance: Evidence from the Banking Industry," *Journal of Political Economy* 101, No. 2 (April 1993): 299–326.

[16] Sharmistha Mukherjee, "Cavendish Industries gets a turnaround after takeover by JK Tyre," *The Economic Times*, April 15, 2017, https://economictimes.indiatimes.com/industry/auto/news/tyres/cavendish-industries-gets-a-turn-around-after-take-over-by-jk-tyre/articleshow/58187747.cms.

[17] ETMarkets.com, "Monnet Ispat Surges 17% On Takeover Buzz," *The Economic Times,* June 21, 2017, https://economictimes.indiatimes.com/markets/stocks/news/monnet-ispat-surges-7-on-takeover-buzz/articleshow/59247339.cms.

Annual Report of the Council of Economic Advisers of Australia in 1985[18] concluded that takeovers stimulate effective corporate management and maximise the shareholder wealth of target companies.[19] Further, the process of takeovers helps in identifying the potential of such companies.[20]

It would, therefore, not be unreasonable to conclude that takeovers are beneficial and contribute significantly to the economy, whether it is in the form of creation of synergy between two corporations, or increasing the aggregate firm value of acquiring and target companies, or reviving target companies from poor economic conditions by infusing the necessary investment.[21] Takeovers, therefore, should be allowed to operate in an investment-friendly market.

Mandatory Offer Requirement—A Mistaken Ideal with Mismatched Efficiency

The European Parliament and the Council brought about the Takeover Directive 2004/25 with the intent to safeguard minority shareholders from oppressive conduct on the part of controlling shareholders and to preserve the rights of such shareholders in the event of a takeover. MOR, or Mandatory Bid Rule, is one of the principal means by which the concerns of minority shareholders of an offeree company are addressed, not only in the EU's Directive but also in the laws of India,[22] England,[23] Singapore,[24] South Africa[25] and many other jurisdictions.

Despite these intentions, the presence of MOR in its current form as a preventive measure in takeover regulation is unfair and redundant. The primary aim of MOR—i.e., to provide the right to exit to the minority

---

[18] "Annual Report of the Council of Economic Advisers," Federal Reserve Bank of St. Louis, January 19, 1985, https://fraser.stlouisfed.org/files/docs/publications/ERP/1985/ERP_ARCEA_1985.pdf.

[19] Lyman Johnson, "Corporate Takeovers And Corporations: Who Are They For?" Washington and Lee Law Review 43, (January 1986): 781.

[20] C.S. Balasubramaniam, "An Appraisal of SEBI Takeover Code, 2011," SEBI and Corporate Laws 110, (December 2011): 98.

[21] Mark L. Mitchell, "The Value of Corporate Takeovers," *Financial Analysts Journal* 47, No. 1 (January–February 1991): 21–31.

[22] Securities and Exchange Board of India (Substantial Acquisition of Shares and Takeovers) Regulations, 2011, regs. 3 and 4.

[23] The City Code on Takeovers and Mergers, 1968, rule 9 (UK).

[24] Singapore Code on Take-Overs and Mergers, 2007, rule 14.

[25] Securities Regulation Code on Takeovers and Mergers, rule 8.

shareholders in the event of change in control—is solely based on the presumption that the new controlling shareholder will be oppressive in its policies towards the incumbent shareholders. It seems a little odd that the benefit of doubt is not given to the potential acquirer for directing the operations of the target company,[26] inviting imposition of financial burdens. In *Re Astec*,[27] the Chancery Court of England held that mere concerns of a future breach of fiduciary duty by directors cannot provide a claim for prevention of oppression. Instead, there has to be an actual abuse of power by the shareholders, such as altering the Memorandum or the Articles of Association,[28] to warrant an action against the oppressive controlling shareholder. The author proposes that MOR should be available as a remedial measure in takeover regulations, rather than as a preventive measure, because the conduct of oppression, being a question of law, cannot be entirely presumed.

It is pertinent to note that, while the minority shareholders invoking MOR as a consequence of the oppressive conduct of the acquirer will eventually increase the financial burden upon the acquirer, it will not deter them initially from investing in target companies, hence increasing the incidence of corporate takeovers. On the other hand, the principle of equal treatment cannot be taken as the rationale for sharing of control premiums as elaborated at a later stage by the author. The European Court of Justice has also held[29] that the equality principle cannot be inferred, despite there being an express provision of Mandatory Bid Rule[30] in the Directive to that effect, to impose an obligation upon the investor to share the control premium with the minority shareholders as a preventive measure.

Even when one turns a blind eye to the inherent flaws of the MOR rationale, the mechanism of MOR and its implementation suffer from serious defects, which in turn render MOR ineffective in providing protection to the interests of minority shareholders. In case of investment made in a target company, wherein the incumbent controller is in financial distress, the controller will be desperate to transfer the control, howsoever low the price of the stake may be. The price of the bid offered to the minority shareholders is generally based on the price offered to the

---

[26] Nicholas Jennings, "Mandatory Bids Revisited," *Journal of Corporate Law Studies* 5, Part 1 (April 2005): 43.

[27] In *Re Astec* (1999) BCC 59.

[28] G. K. Yarrow, "Shareholder Protection, Compulsory Acquisition and the Efficiency of the Takeover Process," *The Journal of Industrial Economics* 34, No. 1 (September 1985): 4.

[29] Audiolux S.A. v. Bruxelles Lambert SA, Case C-101/08, E.C.J. (2009).

[30] Directive 2004/25/EC on Takeover Bids (see n. 1).

incoming controller, which in this case will be severely less; hence, minority shareholders will suffer at the cost of MOR. The Australian Securities and Investment Commission (ASIC) considered the same parameter while rejecting including the Mandatory Bid Rule in the takeover regulations in Australia.[31]

In addition to this, the "trigger limit"[32] of MOR—i.e., "control"—is an immensely broad concept, and an all-encompassing definition of control is practically impossible owing to the emerging nature[33] and dynamism of corporate control; however, the blurred domains of control are some of the decisive factors contributing to the inefficacies of MOR.

Upon investing in a target company, the real question which arises is whether the investor is in a position to exercise "effective control"[34] over the target company; if yes, then the investor has to fulfil the MOR. The parameters of "control" vary across jurisdictions, with most of them opting for a numerical threshold (European Union, England, Singapore), some opting for qualitative criterion of control dependant on facts of each case (Brazil), and others opting for a combination of the above parameters (India, Indonesia, Spain, South Africa).[35] Due to the prevalence of dispersed shareholding patterns in most countries, control can be exercised even without the shareholder owning a majority of shares or having power to elect a majority of directors in the company (popularly known as "*de facto* control"),[36] thereby reducing the significance of percentage threshold. The qualitative criterion, however, such as directing and managing the company[37] or controlling the management or policy decisions,[38] gives too much latitude to the courts to interpret control, and an inconsistency in the judicial decisions is often observed as a consequence.

---

[31] Justin Mannolini, "The Mandatory Bid Rule?" *Keeping Good Companies* 52, (November 2000): 592.

[32] Securities and Exchange Board of India (Substantial Acquisition of Shares and Takeovers) Regulations, 2011, reg. 2(e).

[33] David C. Bayne, "A Philosophy of Corporate Control," *University of Pennsylvania Law Review* 112, No. 1 (November 1963): 29, http://www.jstor.org/stable/3310655.

[34] Shubhkam Ventures (I) Private Limited v. SEBI, 99 SCL 159 (2010).

[35] Umakanth Varottil, "Concept of Control," (see n. 5).

[36] International Financial Reporting Standards, standard 10.

[37] Brazilian Corporations Law (No. 6, 404/76), sec. 116.

[38] Securities and Exchange Board of India (Substantial Acquisition of Shares and Takeovers) Regulations, 2011, reg. 2(1)(e).

Negative control[39] has further contributed towards deepening the controversy of corporate control. It is a reactive[40] power exercised by the investor, either in the form of veto[41] or affirmative voting rights through shareholder purchase agreement, to unilaterally block certain resolutions of the target company; however, the recognition of negative control is incidental to the kinds of decisions in which such rights are guaranteed. If the negative rights are allowed in the basic re-organisation scheme of the target company, then it may act affirmatively towards establishing control.[42]

Sometimes a lack of intention in acquiring control is given preference for ascertaining control, irrespective of the fact that negative rights have accentuated the position of investor as a controller.[43] Due attention should be paid to the intention of the investor in acquiring control while determining the question of MOR as it helps the court to determine conclusively whether the investor should be burdened with MOR or not and further helps to reduce the inefficacies associated with it. There are instances when the role of an investor, having the shareholding well below the trigger limit, is held to be that of a controller by virtue of the voting rights granted, although the investor did not intend to acquire control of the corporation in the first place. The Pennington Committee, responsible for initial takeover reforms in the EU, in its report, also recommended "intention to acquire control" as one of the pre-requisites for triggering MOR.[44]

With the emergence of the concept of corporate control in contemporary times, there cannot be a straightjacket formula to determine control as the trigger limit of MOR. The persisting ambiguity of corporate control coupled with new standards being devised by courts, like the presence of an investor's quorum rights in board meetings as determinant of control (Jet-Etihad deal),[45] grants adequate leeway to corporations to structure their transactions so as to avoid compliance with MOR, thereby

---

[39] Third Point L.L.C. v. Ruprecht, No. 9469-V.C.P., slip op. (Del. Ch. May 2, 2014); In re GE Chemical Company S.A., 2007 SCC Online SEBI 78.

[40] In re MCX Stock Exchange Ltd., 2010 SCC Online SEBI 10 (India).

[41] Zohar Goshen and Assaf Hamdani, "Corporate Control and Idiosyncratic Vision," *Yale Law Journal* 125, Issue 3 (January 2016): 614.

[42] Rhodia S.A. v. SEBI, 34 SCL 597 (SAT 2001) (India); FCT v Commonwealth Aluminium Corporation Ltd., 143 CLR 646 (1980).

[43] Sandip Save v. SEBI, 41 SCL 47 (SAT 2003) (India).

[44] Robert R. Pennington, "Report on Takeover and Other Bids: EU Commission - Working Document XI/56/74-E.," (1974) http://aei.pitt.edu/33743/.

[45] In re Tailwinds Ltd., 2014 SCC Online SEBI 283 (India).

making MOR's presence as a measure of protection of minority rights an exercise in futility.

Mandatory Offer Requirement Decelerating Corporate Takeovers in the Economy

As indicated above, the inclusion of MOR as a central theme of takeover regulations has been justified on two grounds—providing "right to exit"[46] to the minority shareholders and ensuring "fair and equitable treatment" of shareholders.[47] The intended aims of the MOR have inevitably impaired the market for corporate control, however, thereby impeding corporate takeovers in the process. The nature of MOR decelerating corporate takeovers comes in conflict with one of the primary purposes with which the takeover laws are enacted—i.e., not to impede takeovers in economy.[48]

Upon the acquisition of control of the target company, the investor is obliged to extend an open offer to the remaining shareholders, the price of which has to be either the one which is offered to the controlling shareholder[49] or the one that would be determined in accordance with the takeover regulations[50] (based on the share price offered to the controlling shareholder), depending upon the domestic laws. Irrespective of the intention to acquire control, the investor is compelled to arrange a substantial amount of money for the rest of the bid either from loans or by issuing equity.[51] This in itself is a hectic process and may require necessary clearances. It has to be done while keeping in mind the effect this transaction would have on the income statement of the investor. The whole arduous process is bound to create a chilling effect on the takeovers in the economy as the potential acquirer may reconsider its decision of

---

[46] Defriez, Button, and Bolton, *A Practitioner's Guide to the City Code on Takeovers and Mergers*, (see n. 6), 96–97.
[47] Directive 2004/25/EC on Takeover Bids (see n. 1).
[48] The City Code on Takeover and Mergers, sec. 2.
[49] Directive 2004/25/EC on Takeover Bids, art. 5(5) (see n. 1).
[50] Securities and Exchange Board of India (Substantial Acquisition of Shares and Takeovers) Regulations, 2011, reg. 8.
[51] Shardul S. Shroff, "Major Recast of Takeover Code," *Livemint*, July 20, 2010, accessed on November 18, 2017, http://www.livemint.com/2010/07/19224733/Major-recast-of-takeover-code.html.

making the mandatory bid altogether.[52] The acquisition costs may well be above the returns that the investor anticipates post-takeover, and the margin of private benefits accruing to the investor will be relatively less. This in itself has the potential to deter the investors from making substantial investments in target companies, thereby preventing many efficient and value-increasing transactions[53] that a takeover may entail, considering the vital role it plays in the economy. The Securities and Exchange Board of India has time and again given relaxations regarding the open-offer obligations, whether it is to reduce the financial burden on the companies engaged in the acquisition[54] or to facilitate investment by banks in distressed companies.[55]

Further, the obligation of extending the offer to the rest of the shareholders of the target company entails a lot of risk upon the investor and his/her company. If the bid made by the investor for the shares of the minority shareholders is not accepted by them, the customer confidence in the investor company is likely to deteriorate in the period accompanying the unsuccessful takeover. This may eventually lead the share prices to fall, having a severe impact on the profitability of the bidding enterprise. The bidder's shareholder wealth is ultimately destroyed in a failed takeover attempt,[56] which is also reflected in the capital market's reaction following the announcement of a takeover bid.[57] A failed takeover by

---

[52] Thomas Papadopoulos, "The Mandatory Provisions of the EU Takeover Bid Directive and Their Deficiencies," *Law and Financial Markets Review* 1, Issue 6 (November 2007): 528.

[53] Simone M. Sepe, "Private Sale of Corporate Control: Why the European Mandatory Bid Rule is Inefficient," *Arizona Legal Studies Discussion Paper* No. 10–29, (August 2010).

[54] ET Bureau, "SEBI may consider L&T's exemption of open offer plea," *The Economic Times*, January 28, 2009, accessed January 28, 2009, https://economictimes.indiatimes.com/tech/software/sebi-may-consider-lts-exemption-of-open-offer-plea/articleshow/4039432.cms.

[55] ETMarkets.com, "SEBI lets banks to buy stakes in indebted companies without open offer," *The Economic Times,* accessed August 16, 2017, https://economictimes.indiatimes.com/markets/stocks/news/sebi-lets-banks-to-buy-stakes-in-indebted-companies-without-open-offer/articleshow/60084971.cms.

[56] Karyn L. Neuhauser, Wallace N. Davidson III, and John L. Glascock, "An analysis of failed takeover attempts and merger cancellations," *International Journal of Managerial Finance* 7, Issue 4, (2011): 347–76, http://www.emeraldinsight.com/doi/abs/10.1108/17439131111166375.

[57] Sayan Chatterjee, "Sources of Value in Takeovers: Synergy or Restructuring—Implications for Target and Bidder Firms," *Strategic Management Journal* 13, Issue 4 (May 1992): 267–86.

Helphire, a healthcare firm of Bath, England, costing the firm £1m, is a clear example of the above proposition.[58]

The rationale of MOR is firmly grounded on the equality principle, which witnesses an erroneous application when it comes to evaluating a fair and equitable treatment of shareholders. The idea of equal treatment, as devised by Sir Ivor Jennings, emphasises the fact that similar treatment should be guaranteed to similarly situated people and vice-versa. MOR, however, provides that the same amount of control premium be paid to the shareholders, whether it is the controlling entity or the minority; this can essentially prove to be derogation from the principle of equal treatment. The proposition of the author is not intended to discriminate between minority and majority shareholders; the suggestion here is that, apart from being a shareholder incurring maximum liability in a corporation, the controlling shareholder spends time and effort, prior to the acquirer's bid, to negotiate the best possible prices for the company, unlike the rest of the shareholders. MOR, however, ensures that the minority shareholders benefit unduly from the efforts of the controller and are paid the same control premium regardless of the fact that it is being paid at the cost of the potential acquirer's private profits.[59]

Roscoe Pound's theory of social engineering says that the balance between two competing interests should be such that there is maximisation of competing interests and minimisation of friction/waste; however, balance between the protection of the minority's interests and the economic interests is not desirable as it further skews the takeover regulations in favour of minority protection, proving detrimental to the economy.[60] Escalation of acquisition costs for the potential acquirer due to MOR is one of the instrumental reasons for the slowing down of the takeover activity in the market. It is high time that a "pro-minority" and "anti-takeover" protective device like MOR be given some reformation in its rigid mechanism and a harmonious balance between the two competing interests is adopted in order to mitigate the adverse effects of MOR on the economy.

---

[58] "Helphire's Abandoned Takeover Costs £1m," Bath Chronicle, accessed January 17, 2007, http://www.lexisnexis.com/hottopics/lnacademic/Default.asp.

[59] Luca Enriques, "The Mandatory Bid Rule in the Takeover Directive: Harmonization without Foundation?" *European Company and Financial Law Review* 1, (2004).

[60] Shane Tulloch, "Takeover Regulation in New Zealand: Policy for Competitive Advantage," *Auckland University Law Review* 7, Issue 2 (1993): 270.

Conclusion and Suggestions

Although MOR is prevalent in most jurisdictions' takeover regulations, its presence neither effectively safeguards the interests of minority shareholders nor proves beneficial to the economy in the long run. The only reason that justifies its inclusion in the takeover law is the advancement of corporate democracy by equal treatment of shareholders in the event of a takeover. The European Court of Justice has also declined to deduce the principle of equality of shareholders from the EU Takeover Directive, despite there being an express provision of MOR to that effect, and called for harmonisation of competing interests taking into account the considerable benefits of corporate takeovers.[61] There does, however, have to be some mechanism for combating the oppression of minority shareholders of a target company, and MOR cannot be completely done away with. Its implementation can be instead invoked as a remedial measure by the minority shareholders in the form of financial sanctions upon the investor when there is any actual abuse of power by the potential acquirer, which, being a question of law, will be decided by courts. Moreover, instead of including MOR in the takeover codes of respective countries, it is more feasible to leave it to the discretion of the target company by incorporating it into their foundational documents like memoranda and articles of association, which has incidentally been adopted by the Takeover Regulations of Finland in 2014.[62]

Further, the launch of a takeover bid can also be made subject to shareholder approval, necessitating the presence of a special majority of shareholders so as to determine whether the bid is actually and seemingly beneficial to the target company. This approach might be quite restrictive to successful takeovers, but it will do away with the anti-investor nature of MOR and ensure the preservation of minority interests as the investor will not be obliged to offer a bid to the rest of the shareholders.

As far as the efficiency of MOR is concerned, the domains of corporate control cannot, in any case, be defined for the purposes of takeover; yet, there are certain inherent flaws which, if tackled properly, can optimise the functioning of MOR. Firstly, there has to be a legislative enactment calling for a distinction between positive or initiation rights (e.g., tabling a proposal in the shareholders' meeting) and negative or veto/affirmative voting rights. The investor conferred with only initiation rights in the course of investment should be considered for the purposes of control,

[61] Audiolux S.A. v. Bruxelles Lambert SA, Case C-101/08, E.C.J. (2009).

[62] The Helsinki Takeover Code, 2014, part VII (a).

disregarding negative rights as there will always be a presumption that the purpose of these rights is protection of the investor's rights; however, this position can always be misconstrued to be that of control exercised through blocking or reacting to management or policy decisions. In addition to that, the intention of the acquirer seeking control in the target company should be given consideration while determining the control threshold for MOR. The use of terms like "essential management decisions" or "major policy decisions" should be avoided in the investor-investee agreement as regards the decisions wherein veto/affirmative vote exists, so as to restrain the courts from exercising unfettered discretion while determining the issue of control. The application of these principles cannot totally eliminate the deficiencies concerning MOR, but they can certainly be a step, depending upon the condition of domestic corporate and securities regimes, towards a harmonious balance between protection of the minority's interests and economic interests advanced by corporate takeovers.

CHAPTER VI

COMPETITION LAW CLIMATE CHANGE IN INDIA—WILL IT HEAT UP THE M&A LANDSCAPE?

AVANI MISHRA

Abstract

This essay is focused on highlighting the neoteric changes in competition law framework and its implementation in the year 2017. The essay is loosely divided into three parts, progressing from a general perspective on the need for competition law regulation towards more specific aspects of exemptions and relaxed regulatory dimensions this year. The first part assesses the interplay between competition law and merger transactions, including considerations driving M&A and determining how a merger is likely to harm competition. The second part highlights the shift in the Competition Commission of India's viewpoint towards large players forming a post-merger dominant entity by drawing a distinction between the Lafarge-Holcim deal of 2015 and the Idea-Vodafone merger approval of 2017. The third aspect of this essay relates to analysing general and industry-specific exemptions granted in the last few months and their impact on sustaining the upward momentum of India's growth story.

Introduction

It was the year 1305 in England. Much to the disadvantage of the peasantry, the prices of bread and corn were soaring, as ships were stopped and grains hoarded by large suppliers. It was then that King Edward ordained what is presumably one of the earliest directions regulating trade combinations in the following words: "That no merchant or other shall make Confederacy, Conspiracy, Coin, Imagination, or Murmur, or Evil

Device in any point that may turn to the Impeachment, Disturbance, Defeating or Decay of the said Staples, or of anything that to them pertaineth, or may pertain."[1] Centuries later, the same protectionist sentiment echoes as more than 110 countries now have anti-trust laws in place, and at least 100 of such laws include merger control, making competition law restraints an important discussion for every M&A deal.[2]

This essay, while highlighting neoteric changes in the competition law framework and implementation in the year 2017, focuses on the outlook for M&A in India from the lens of anti-trust. Complementing the research are cases, administrative perspectives and notifications issued in the last few months—all convergent on the aim of escalating India's growth story.

Competition Law and M&A in India

With one foot grounded in a strong commercial law regime and the other fervently striding to embrace globalisation, India has achieved a 30-rank elevation to finish at the 100th spot in the Ease of Doing Business Index 2017 (the highest jump that any country has ever made in this index).[3] The regulatory regime for doing business in India attracts various laws such as the Companies Act, the Takeover Code and the Income Tax Act; however, the focus of the Competition Act, 2002 (the Competition Act) is quite different as it is predominantly concerned with maintaining fair competition in the marketplace, not as an end in itself, but as a way of maximising consumer welfare. Mergers ideally involve the coming together of two or more companies to form a new company. Similarly, acquisition or takeover relates to an entity acquiring control over another, which may be friendly or hostile. A joint venture is another mechanism enabling two or more companies to unite for a specific purpose or duration. In the competition law sense, horizontal mergers between similar enterprises presumably present greater danger as firms may limit output or increase prices.[4] The regulatory body, the Competition Commission of India (CCI), established under the Competition Act, 2002 and replacing the Monopolies and Restrictive Trade Practices Act, 1969, aims to

---

[1] Barry Hawk, *International Antitrust Law and Policy* (Juris Publishing Inc., 2004), 17.

[2] Richard Whish and David Bailey, *Competition Law* (Oxford, 2012, 7th ed.), 812.

[3] Joe C. Mathew, "Ease of Doing Business 2018 rankings: India jumps 30 points to reach top-100 club," *Business Today,* November 1, 2017, http://www.businesstoday.in/current/economy-politics/ease-of-doing-business-ranking-2018-india-rank-world-bank/story/263003.html.

[4] Richard Whish and David Bailey, *Competition Law*, 818.

delicately balance the opposing positive goals—promoting freedom of trade while sustaining competition. This is done through a pre-merger notification of all combinations above prescribed thresholds that will have an appreciable adverse effect within the relevant market. It is interesting to note that, out of 255 applications filed for approval since 2015, no application has been rejected on any ground.[5] While this further indicates the inclination towards promoting foreign collaborations, restructuring and freedom of trade, it also raises several questions about what the true standard for processing an application is, considering the absence of clear legislative and judicial benchmarks.

Interplay of Competition Law and M&A Transactions

Considerations Driving Mergers and Acquisitions

With rapid technological changes and lowering of trade and tariff barriers globally, the world has become a single geographical market giving rise to increased opportunity, fierce competition and greater efforts required for survival. One of the most common reasons for this is attaining economies of scale as marginal costs decrease when the production is undertaken on a larger scale, thereby distributing the high cost. The approval of the combination of Mumbai International Airport Ltd. with four major oil-players in the Indian market for reducing aviation turbine fuel costs and improving distribution infrastructure of turbine fuel through corporate synergies between leading oil companies is one such example.[6]

Other reasons may include availability of cheaper raw material, strategic moves for accelerating growth—such as the Vodafone-Idea deal—emerging as a result of threat by a new entrant, and imitating competitor's moves as indicated by the speculated merger of Bharti Airtel with Tata to help close the gap that the Vodafone-Idea deal is likely to create.[7] Tech Mahindra's acquisition of Satyam at a time when the latter

---

[5] Data accessed from http://www.cci.gov.in/10 (last visited on November 24, 2017).

[6] Order under section 31(1) of the Competition Act, 2002, Combination Registration No. C-2014/04/164 (2014), September 29, 2014, http://www.cci.gov.in/sites/default/files/faq/C-2014-04-164_0.pdf.

[7] Kalyan Parbat, "Merger with Tata to help Bharti Airtel close gap with Vodafone-Idea," *Economic Times*, July 11, 2017, https://economictimes.indiatimes.com/news/company/corporate-trends/merger-with-tata-to-help-bharti-airtel-close-gap-with-vodafone-idea/articleshow/59536303.cms.

was under distress is a good example of inorganic growth. Moreover, foreign firms eyeing Indian markets may diversify operations across distances through acquisitions or joint ventures to capitalise on the existing abilities of an Indian firm, such as the French company Lafarge's entry by acquiring the cement unit of Tata Steel.

The Argument for Merger Control

Competition laws aim to curtail abuse of dominance of power in a market. A question may be raised at this point as to why the existing framework of competition law aims to control the "possibility" of abuse even before the new entity comes into play as conduct should be punished on "actual" abuse of market power. An explanation is that merger control is not simply about preventing future abuses: it is also about maintaining competitive market structures which lead to better outcomes for consumers by inhibiting wealth and resource concentration.[8] Moreover, it has been held that, considering the remote possibility of getting direct evidence in the case of an anti-competitive collusion, the existence of an agreement can be inferred from a number of coincidences and indicia which, taken together, may, in the absence of any other plausible explanation, constitute evidence of the existence of an agreement.[9] The existing anti-trust framework is, therefore, forward-looking, aimed at assessing the future effects of a merger on the national market and consumers. This predictive nature while assessing approval under section 6 is evidently different from the process of assessing conduct pursuant to an agreement under section 19, where the CCI undertakes detailed investigation of behaviour of enterprises to determine whether the conduct amounted to an anti-competitive abuse by a dominant enterprise.

Determining Whether a Merger is Likely to Harm Competition Significantly

While firms in their public announcements may proclaim that they are becoming the dominant leader in a certain market to sway shareholders, such pronouncements are likely to attract the attention of the CCI as it is concerned with possible adverse effects of such market domination. Forms

---

[8] Case T- 102/96, Gencor v. Commission, [1999] ECR II- 753, [1999] 4 CMLR 971, para 106.

[9] In re: Alleged Cartelization by Steel Producers, MRTP Case: RTPE No. 09 of 2008.

I and II under the CCI (Procedure in regard to the Transaction of Business relating to Combinations) Regulations, 2011 require furnishing information on more than 80 points by parties to the combination such as details of series of constituent transactions leading to the combination and the sequence, explaining the purpose of the combination (including the business objective and/or economic rationale for each of the parties to the combination and how they are intended to be achieved). The CCI also mandates furnishing details of the sector overview that requires parties to a combination to state whether they provide similar or identical or substitutable products or services, whether any of the parties to the combination have direct or indirect shareholding and/or control over (an)other enterprise(s) engaged in: (a) production, distribution or trading of similar/identical/substitutable products or provision of similar/identical/substitutable services; and/or (b) any activity relating to the production, supply, distribution, storage, sale and service or trade in products or provision of services which is at different stages or levels of the production chain in which any other party to the combination is involved. Although the multitude of details help the CCI in forming an opinion on whether the combination is likely to cause appreciable adverse effects on competition, the qualitative weight of each parameter (purpose, nature of products, production and distribution control, economic rationale, etc.) is relatively unknown, resulting in a lot of room for a party and its legal counsels to argue in favour of the economic value and efficiencies created by the proposed transaction.

The Lafarge-Holcim Forced Divestiture—Have the Winds Changed Since Then?

In 2015, rival firms Lafarge and Swiss-based Holcim merged to form the world's largest cement company, LafargeHolcim. Lafarge had been operating in India through its acquisition of the cement unit of Tata Steels in 1999, while Holcim's entities included ACC and Ambuja Cements; however, the combined entity was required to seek approval from competition regulators in individual jurisdictions. In India, the CCI strongly opposed the combination due to the likelihood of an appreciable adverse effect on competition as the entity would have acquired a combined market share of 41% and an aggregate installed capacity of 37%. It also considered barriers to entry in the cement industry and the large difference from the second biggest player, Ultratech (17%). Instead of refusing approval, the CCI proposed a modification that included selling off all assets in Eastern areas of Jharkhand and Chhattisgarh—the jewels in Lafarge's India business, with high market shares and an ecosystem that included limestone reserves and grinding facilities.[10]

Two years later, the largest-ever merger deal in India is proposed as telecom players Idea and Vodafone decided to unite. The combined market share of 35%, making it the largest mobile operating network, received an unconditional approval from the CCI.[11] Although the market conditions across two sectors as diverse as telecom and cement may not be comparable, it is noteworthy that the coming together of two giants to become the biggest player in an essential consumer segment did not lead to concerns being expressed by the CCI regarding any appreciable adverse effect. Although significant barriers to entry coupled with high post-merger market shares were the determinative factors in considering a modification in the Lafarge-Holcim deal, the aspects were accepted internationally, indicating that the significant barriers to entry in this case—the huge investment requirement in the telecom sector, the reputation of the two players and the reduced incentive of new players to enter the mobile-network market[12]—were not significant concerns for the CCI. This shift in the viewpoint of the regulator and the recent notifications in 2017 are largely aimed at accelerating the scale of M&A activity in India.

Since the Lafarge-Holcim case, no major modifications have been suggested in Phase 2[13] of enquiry by the CCI. Cases with clauses like non-compete restrictions[14] have usually been sent back for modification (such as removal of a "lock-in period" and "minimum-shareholding" to promote

---

[10] Order under section 31(7) of the Competition Act, 2002, Combination Registration No. C-2014/07/190, March 30, 2015, http://www.cci.gov.in/sites/default/files/C-2014-07-190_0.pdf.

[11] "CCI approves $23 billion Vodafone India-Idea deal: Sources," *Times of India*, July 24, 2017, https://timesofindia.indiatimes.com/business/india-business/cci-approves-23-billion-vodafone-india-idea-deal-sources/articleshow/59741011.cms.

[12] Order under section 31(7) of the Competition Act, 2002, Combination Registration No. C-2014/07/190, March 30, 2015, http://www.cci.gov.in/sites/default/files/C-2014-07-190_0.pdf.

[13] Phase 1 refers to the deal being approved within 30 working days as provided by the Competition Act. Getting approval within Phase I implies that the deal would not be subject to detailed scrutiny. Transactions where there are *prima facie* concerns that they would adversely impact competition are taken into Phase II for an in-depth scrutiny.

[14] The standards for upholding a non-compete restriction have been laid down by the CCI in its Guidance on Non-Compete Restrictions, 2011, accessed on October 16, 2017, http://cci.gov.in/sites/default/files/Non-Compete/Guidance_Note.pdf.

free transfer of shares[15]), and, as suggested above, no case has been rejected by the CCI thus far.

Respite in Filings—Removal of the Compulsory 30-day Notification Window

Section 5 enshrines that parties to the acquisition, being the acquirer and the enterprise, whose control, shares, voting rights or assets have been acquired or are being acquired jointly, crossing the prescribed thresholds mentioned therein is a combination of such enterprises. The parties to the combination have to provide a pre-transaction notice to the CCI disclosing the details of the proposed combination within 30 days of the approval of the proposal relating to merger or amalgamation by the board of directors of the enterprises, along with execution of any agreement or other document for acquisition of the combination in case of a merger/amalgamation. If the parties to the combination fail to notify the CCI within 30 days of the approval or execution, the CCI could impose a penalty on such parties extending up to 1% of the total turnover or of the assets, whichever is higher.[16] It is striking that in three major deals of the year 2014–15 a heavy penalty of Rs. 3–5 crores had been imposed merely for the procedural inadequacy in filing the requisite notice with CCI within 30 days. This includes General Electric (GE)'s acquisition of the renewable power business of Alstom SA, where the CCI imposed a penalty of Rs. 5 crores on GE while defining notification to stock exchanges as the trigger date for reckoning the 30 days' period.[17] By virtue of a notification issued on June 29, 2017, however, this requirement for filing notice has been relaxed subject to compliance with the provisions of section 6(2A).[18] Section 6(2A) mandates that a scheme of combination would not come into existence before the lapse of 210 days from filing the notice with CCI

[15] Order under section 31(1) of the Competition Act, 2002, Combination Registration No. C-2014/04/164, September 29, 2014, http://www.cci.gov.in/sites/default/files/faq/C-2014-04-164_0.pdf.

[16] Competition Act 2002, No. 12 of 2003, sec. 43A.

[17] "Schedule 1, Merger Control Exemptions Expanded- Better Late Than Never!" Nishith Desai Associates, April 18, 2017 http://www.nishithdesai.com/fileadmin/user_upload/Html/Hotline/170713_H_SCHEDULE1.html.

[18] Notification No. S.O. 2039(E), Competition Commission of India, June 29, 2017, http://www.cci.gov.in/sites/default/files/notification/S.O.%202039%20%28E%29%20-%2029th%20June%202017.pdf.

or granting of approval by CCI under section 31(1)[19], whichever is earlier. Like the GE case, most mergers are complex transactions requiring multiple filings with regulatory authorities, and there is an ambiguity in setting the trigger date for competition law purposes. Under the new exemption granted, all that the parties need to ensure is that the provisions of section 6(2A) are complied with before closing the deal, and thus there is no need to notify the CCI within 30 days of the triggering event.

Boost to Small Industries M&A—The *deminimis* Exemption Threshold Expanded

As mentioned above, combinations with transaction values over a certain threshold are under the increased obligation of legal costs, waiting time and unpredictability associated with getting a nod from the CCI. In line with its goal of furthering the ease of doing business in the country, the Government of India on March 27, 2017 (March 2017 Notification) decided to introduce a wider *deminimis* exemption than that in the 2016 notification.[20] In the erstwhile notification, the exemption was applicable to certain types of combinations, including those in the nature of acquisition, as understood by the use of the expression "enterprise whose control, shares, voting rights or assets were being acquired." This denied the advantage of the exemption to a combination in the nature of a merger or amalgamation. Under the new notification, however, this incongruity stands clarified, the exemption now being provided for a period of five years to any enterprise being party to any form of combination covered in section 5 if the value of the assets being acquired/merged/amalgamated/ taken control over is not more than Rs. 3.5 billion in India or if the turnover does not exceed Rs. 10 billion.[21]

---

[19] Competition Act 2002, sec. 31- Orders of Commission on certain combinations - (1) Where the Commission is of the opinion that any combination does not, or is not likely to, have an appreciable adverse effect on competition, it shall, by order, approve that combination including the combination in respect of which a notice has been given under sub-section (2) of section 6.

[20] Notification no. S.O. 988(E), Competition Commission of India, March 27, 2017, published in *The Gazette of India*, March 29, 2017, http://www.cci.gov.in/sites/default/files/notification/S.O.%20988%20%28E%29%20and%20S.O.%20989%28E%29.pdf.

[21] Notification no. S.O. 674(E), Competition Commission of India, published in *The Gazette of India*, March 4, 2016, http://www.cci.gov.in/sites/default/files/notification/SO%20673%28E%29-674%28E%29-675%28E%29.pdf.

Much-needed Liberalisation of Rules for Calculation of Assets

Explanation (c) to section 5 states that the "value of assets shall be determined by taking the book value of the assets as shown, in the audited books of account of the enterprise." The repercussion of this oddity was that, regardless of whether 1% or 100% of the total assets were being taken over, the calculation would include the book value of the entire assets. The March 2017 Notification also clarifies, however, that the scope of assets relevant for calculation of financial thresholds shall include only those being acquired: "Where a portion of an enterprise or division or business is being acquired, taken control of, merged or amalgamated with another enterprise, the value of assets of the said portion or division or business and or attributable to it, shall be the relevant assets and turnover to be taken into account for the purpose of calculating the thresholds under section 5 of the Act."[22]

The impact of these three provisions can be empirically observed from the significant decrease in the combination approval orders by the CCI after the release of the first notification in March until November 2017. Compared to the108 applications approved by the CCI in the calendar year 2016, as 2017 draws to a close only 28 applications relating to the period after the release of the March 2017 Notification have been approved.[23]

Industry-Specific Exemptions in 2017

Accelerating Mergers in the Banking Sector

Traditionally, banking had been a highly regulated industry in India, and, under the Competition Act, consolidation had only been encouraged pursuant to an investment agreement or a loan agreement for public financial institutions, banks, venture capital funds[24] and other failing banks.[25]

In February 2017, a complaint was filed arguing that the proposed merger of India's biggest national bank—SBI—with four associate banks

[22] Notification no. S.O. 988(E).

[23] As of November 27, 2017, assuming roughly four applications were filed each month, totalling to 28 in eight months (March–November), compared with 108 applications in 2016; thus, roughly nine applications each month. Data accessed from http://www.cci.gov.in/10 (last visited November 27, 2017).

[24] Competition Act, 2002, sec. 6(4).

[25] "Finance Ministry wants loss-making banks, insurers out of CCI ambit: MCA," *The Hindu Business Line,* September 3, 2012.

(State Bank of Bikaner & Jaipur, State Bank of Mysore, State Bank of Travancore and Bhartiya Mahila Bank) was in violation of the letter and spirit of the Competition Act on the ground that the real purpose and intent of the proposed merger was to create a monopoly and destroy competition.[26]

Following the notification released on August 30, 2017,[27] however, SBI does not need approval from CCI for the merger, despite the resultant combination becoming the market leader in the banking sector, with the second-largest lender, ICICI Bank, being relegated to a size which would be one-fourth of SBI in terms of total deposits and advances.[28]

Another notification has also exempted Regional Rural Banks from seeking approval for combinations for which the Central Government has issued a notification under section 23A(1) of the Regional Rural Banks Act, 1976.[29] It is noteworthy that the CCI had imposed a penalty of Rs. 1 lakh last year for failure to notify regarding the amalgamation between Rajasthan Marudhara Gramin Bank and the State Bank of Bikaner and Jaipur before completion of the deal, despite the compelling argument that the amalgamation was carried out pursuant to directions by the Central Government. With FDI being permitted up to 74% (49% under the automatic route and beyond 49% up to 74% under the Government/approval route) for private banks[30]and demonetisation leading to greater confidence in the banking machinery, these exemptions are in sync with the government's thrust to make India more investor-friendly by setting up an encouraging regulatory framework.

---

[26] Oommen A. Ninan, "SBI-SBT merger likely to be delayed," *The Hindu*, February 19, 2017, http://www.thehindu.com/news/national/kerala/sbisbt-merger-likely-to-be-delayed/article17329851.ece.

[27] Notification no. S.O. 2828(E), Competition Commission of India, published in *The Gazette of India*, August 30, 2017, http://www.cci.gov.in/sites/default/files/notification/Notification%2030.08.2017.pdf.

[28] "SBI merger with associates, BMB exempt from CCI approval," *The Hindu Business Line*, August 21, 2016, http://www.thehindubusinessline.com/money-and-banking/sbi-merger-with-associates-bmb-exempt-from-cci-approval/article9014342.ece.

[29] Notification No. S.O. 2561 (E), Competition Commission of India, published in *The Gazette of India*, August 10, 2017, http://www.cci.gov.in/sites/default/files/notification/Notificiation%20-%2010.08.2017.pdf.

[30] Consolidated FDI Policy of 2017, F. No. 5(1)/2017-FC-1, 5.2.18, Department of Industrial Policy and Promotion, August 28, 2017, http://dipp.nic.in/sites/default/files/CFPC_2017_FINAL_RELEASED_28.8.17.pdf.

Greasing the Wheels for M&A in the Oil and Gas Sector

Even more recently, on November 22, 2017, the Ministry of Corporate Affairs, Government of India (MCA) has issued an exemption to public-sector undertakings for accelerating the mergers in the oil and gas sector, thereby exempting combinations involving Central Public Sector Enterprises in the oil and gas sector, along with their wholly or partly owned subsidiaries, from sections 5 and 6 of the Competition Act for a period of five years.[31]It can hardly be a coincidence, however, that this exemption comes just in time for the sale of the government's 51.11% stake in oil refiner Hindustan Petrol Corporation Limited to the country's largest oil producer Oil and Natural Gas Corporation (popularly known as ONGC), undoubtedly helping it emerge as a strong entity by completely by-passing competition law approvals. Although such an exemption to only public-sector industries can be criticised for hampering freedom of trade of non-state-owned industries, it is in line with the international recommendatory practices on competition assessment, encouraging sunset clauses[32] to advance public policy by giving industry-specific exemptions for short-term durations.[33]

Banking and oil-sector industries are two of the most significant in feeding other industries, especially the manufacturing sector. It is beyond doubt that these moves herald an important step in enhancing the competitiveness of the domestic industry and a likely favourable domino effect on other downstream industries—quite what the Competition Act aims to achieve. It is therefore not surprising that India remains the most competitive country in South Asia, appearing at rank 40 in the global competitiveness ranking of 137 countries by the World Economic Forum.[34]

[31] MCA Notification No. S.O. 3714 (E), Ministry of Corporate Affairs, published in *The Gazette of India*, November 22, 2017, http://www.cci.gov.in/sites/default/files/notification/Notification-22.112017.pdf.

[32] A provision that a law or regulation will expire on a particular date, unless it is reauthorised, or on a statutory requirement to assess the overall impact of legislation or regulation after a certain period.

[33] "Recommended Practices on Competition Assessment," Recommendation 1, Comment 6, International Competition Network, accessed on October 10, 2017, http://www.internationalcompetitionnetwork.org/uploads/library/doc978.pdf.

[34] "The Global Competitiveness Report 2017–2018," World Economic Forum, September 26, 2017, https://www.weforum.org/reports/the-global-competitiveness-report-2017-2018.

Conclusion—Paving the Way for a Robust Yet Liberalised Regime

The real challenge with respect to regulating competition is to minimise the procedural burden to enhance efficiency in the M&A process while ensuring that transactions that could potentially have disastrous effects on competition are not allowed. Although the year 2017 has witnessed significant exemptions to promote M&A activity, the real impact of these exemptions on the economy, competitiveness and efficiency in industries remains to be seen. The recent changes in outlook towards anti-trust in merger transactions are indicative of an encouraging legislative regime. India's rank leap on all major global indexes, and its increase in inbound and outbound transactions, coupled with a burgeoning internet-savvy consumer base, all demonstrate India's immense potential in sustaining this upward momentum in M&A pursuits.